"More than ever, people are searching for purpose and meaning in their lives. Bill is biblical yet culturally connected, and his book is just what the doctor ordered for anyone who wants to satisfy the deepest longing in their heart."

—GREG LAURIE
Senior pastor, Harvest Christian Fellowship

"Bill Ritchie has been a constant source of encouragement and inspiration for many years. Now this book offers biblical proof that satisfaction in life is attainable through an easily understood approach. Bill explains clearly that God wants us to have satisfaction, and he explains how to get it. Thanks, Bill."

—DEL HARRIS
Assistant coach, Dallas Mavericks

"I've seen too many Christians who don't know what it means to live the abundant, satisfying life that Jesus promised us. But Bill Ritchie does. I'm thrilled that Christians will use his book to draw near to God's heart and develop God's character in their own lives."

—LUIS PALAU
Evangelist, broadcaster, and author of *High Definition Life*

"Bill Ritchie brings us perhaps the greatest truth of our time. Satisfaction is from God—and it's guaranteed."

—KAREN KINGSBURY
Bestselling author of *One Tuesday Morning*

"Satisfaction found! This book lives up to its promise. But don't take my word for it—read it!"

—DR. WAYNE CORDEIRO
New Hope Christian Fellowship O'ahu

"Consider what our culture says you need to be satisfied—through advertisements for instance. Then look at the table of contents in Bill Ritchie's *Satisfaction Guaranteed*.

Now choose the path that's both better and smarter, and pursue it wholeheartedly. This book will help you choose wisely, and help you walk the path that pays off both now and for eternity."

—RANDY ALCORN
Bestselling author of *The Treasure Principle* and *Heaven*

"Someone asked, 'When you finish the trip, will you arrive at your desired destination?' In many ways, that is what Bill Ritchie is asking: 'Will the journey to find satisfaction be worth the trip?' For so many, it is not. But when you do it the way Bill says in *Satisfaction Guaranteed,* you will find what so many have missed—satisfaction!"

—H.B. LONDON
Vice President, Church, Clergy and Medical Outreach
Focus on the Family

SATISFACTION

GUARANTEED

BILL RITCHIE

Multnomah® Publishers *Sisters, Oregon*

SATISFACTION GUARANTEED
published by Multnomah Publishers, Inc.
© 2006 by Bill Ritchie
International Standard Book Number: 1-59052-532-9

Published in association with the literary agency of Mark Sweeney & Associates,
28540 Altessa Way, Suite 201, Bonita Springs, FL 34135

Cover design by The Designworks Group, Inc.
Interior design and typset by Katherine Lloyd, The DESK

Unless otherwise indicated, Scripture quotations are from:
The Holy Bible, New King James Version © 1984 by Thomas Nelson, Inc.

Other Scripture quotations are from:
The Holy Bible, New International Version (NIV) © 1973, 1984 by International
Bible Society, used by permission of Zondervan Publishing House
Holy Bible, New Living Translation (NLT) © 1996. Used by permission
of Tyndale House Publishers, Inc. All rights reserved.
The Message by Eugene H. Peterson © 1993, 1994, 1995, 1996, 2000,
2001, 2002 Used by Permission of NavPress Publishing Group
The New Testament in Modern English, Revised Edition (Phillips)
© 1958, 1960, 1972 by J. B. Phillips
Holy Bible, *English Standard Version* (ESV) © 2001 Crossway Bibles,
a division of Good News Publishers. All rights reserved.

Multnomah is a trademark of Multnomah Publishers, Inc.,
and is registered in the U.S. Patent and Trademark Office.
The colophon is a trademark of Multnomah Publishers, Inc.

Printed in the United States of America

For information:
MULTNOMAH PUBLISHERS, INC.
601 N. LARCH STREET • SISTERS, OREGON 97759

Library of Congress Cataloging-in-Publication Data

Ritchie, Bill.
    Satisfaction guaranteed / Bill Ritchie.
        p. cm.
    ISBN 1-59052-532-9
    1. Virtues. 2. Christian life. 3. Satisfaction--Religious aspects--Christianity. I. Title.
BV4630.R58 2006
241'.4--dc22
                                                    2005029513

06 07 08 09 10 11—10 9 8 7 6 5 4 3 2 1

To Betty...
always loving, caring, laughing, encouraging, affirming,
and willing to read, suggest, reread, and suggest some more.

To Jason and Alexa, Geoffrey, Jeff and Lisa...
no longer children, wonderful believing adults, yielded to developing
God's character in their own lives and those of their children.

To Micah, Isaiah, Samuel, Cole, and Lacey...
with lives opening like flowers before us, full of joy, laughter,
curiosity, and enthusiasm for all that lies ahead.

This book about godly character is dedicated
to you who have helped me learn so much about it
as we have shared life's journey together.

Contents

Acknowledgments

Some of my greatest insights into godly character have been gained from my friendship with Pastor John Kennington. Not only does he illustrate a life truly yielded to the Lord in the way he lives, but he willingly shares it with those who cross his path. Our countless lunches together across the years, opening our lives to one another, have been one of God's richest blessings to me. May the Lord continue to bless your life, John.

We all need people who believe in us. Mark Sweeney caught the vision of this project before it even fully congealed. His helpful suggestions and desire to find just the right placement were a real encouragement along the way. Thank you, Mark, for your persistence and friendship.

Working with the folks at Multnomah Publishers has been delightful. People like Doug, Chris, Tim, and so many others have made this project a real joy. I was spurred on by their dedication to and excitement about the book, and feel fortunate to be a part of their team! A heartfelt thanks to each and every one of you!

One of God's greatest gifts in relationship to this book has been working with Larry Libby. I have always admired Larry's unique editorial gifting, and being able to work heart to heart, keyboard to keyboard with him on this project has been a dream come true. His skill as an editor is surpassed only by his love for the Lord and desire to bring out God's best in those with whom he works. Larry, thank you for taking such a personal interest in this book. Indeed, thanks for you, my friend!

Dr. Gale Roid really encouraged me by showing how growth in godly character could be measured. The result of his selfless effort is an instrument that blesses all who use it. Gale, you remind me of Philemon 7: "…the hearts of the saints have been refreshed by you, brother."

Finally, I want to express my heartfelt thanks to the wonderful congregation of believers God has allowed me the joy of leading. Having pastored Crossroads for thirty years now, I continue to be inspired by their desire to know the Lord more completely, love Him more deeply, and live His life more intentionally day by day. Your love and faithfulness challenge me to keep growing in the Lord. You folks are simply the best!

Chapter One

(Can't Get No)

SATISFACTION

Sometimes it's a vague uneasiness.

Sometimes it's a longing that goes bone deep.

Sometimes it's a frustration that boils over into destructive anger.

Sometimes it's a quiet despair that drains you dry and gradually leeches all the color out of your world.

You sense it in the crush of your busiest moments, and feel it even more in those rare intervals of life when everything is quiet and you're all alone. You're not satisfied and you know it. But you don't know why. And you have no idea what to do about it.

When it comes to customer satisfaction, those 800 numbers on the cable channels offer a promise almost as much as a product. They say, "Satisfaction guaranteed," and you know it's a lie. They can't do it; they don't possess it; they can't give it. No product or service on Fox or CNN or the Food Channel will so much as touch that yearning in your gut...in the core of your core...in your heart of hearts. But millions buy the products anyway, just to see if it might be true. Can satisfaction be delivered by UPS 2nd Day Air? Probably not. But then...what if...?

You can't get a large group of people anywhere to agree on most anything. But one thing will get everyone everywhere on the same page every time.

Everybody wants to be satisfied.

It doesn't matter if it's a week-old baby in a bassinet or an old man in a nursing home on a ventilator. It's the same for an Eskimo in a fishing boat in the Arctic Sea as it is for an executive in an Armani suit in a Houston high rise.

You want it, too.

Not the suit…but the pursuit. You want satisfaction. So do I.

Of course we do. It was wired into us at birth. People may disagree about what satisfaction looks like or how to get there, but the fact remains.

Everybody wants to be satisfied.

The world's marketers play off that intense, personal desire in a million ways. And that's where that universal phrase pops up again and again. We've heard it promised ad nauseam but it never goes away. Retailers will use the phrase until the world stops spinning, because they understand our desire, our just-under-the-skin yearning.

Satisfaction guaranteed.

Yeah, right.

Satisfaction guaranteed.

It's ridiculous, of course. It's only sales hype. Marketing buzz. No one can guarantee satisfaction. Not really. Not in real life.

But what if they could? Would you be interested enough to give their claims a second glance?

In this book, I will demonstrate that satisfaction—real, lifelong, soul-sustaining satisfaction—is more than a phantom dream or a will-o'-the-wisp longing that can never find fulfillment. To be even more specific, I will show *you* how to find that which generations innumerable have declared unfindable.

I guarantee it.

But what's more important, *God* guarantees it.

Who knows more about satisfaction than the One who planted that ache and craving—that seemingly unquenchable thirst—in the deep places of the human soul? If *He* can't tell us where and how to find it, then…we might as well call that 800 number and see if the Remote-Control Salad Shooter or that combination hammer/flashlight/cell phone will do the job.

WHAT DOES IT TAKE (REALLY)?

Many would answer that question with the phrase "Just a little bit more."

I'd be satisfied if I had just a little bit more than I have now. Those who assume that money is the source of satisfaction will tell you (if they're honest), *"If only I had more money, then I'd be satisfied."*

Fair enough. But how much is more? What qualifies as *enough*? *More* is exactly that: a larger amount than we currently have. For a five-year-old with a stack of shiny copper pennies, it's just another handful. (And then on to nickels?) For the wage earner who makes $35,000 a year, more may look like $50,000. But $75,000 would bring only temporary satisfaction to the person who is increasing from $50,000 on his way to $100,000!

And the person at two hundred grand? Well, he or she doesn't really have quite enough to achieve that lifestyle just barely out of reach. A little bit more would do it. Maybe.

Satisfaction always seems to be a matter of having just a bit more than we have at the moment.

The same is true with the *stuff* that money buys. The apartment dweller dreams of owning a house (right? have you been there?), while the homeowner with a two-car garage needs a larger garage and a bonus room above it to store all his toys! As the family gets bigger and older, the kids need their space. And college and retirement are right around the corner!

But let's step back and take a good look at this matter of money and satisfaction. The truth is, Americans have never had so much. Never in our history. Think about what we take for granted. We have cable TV with flat-screen monitors to watch our favorite programs in high definition, so it will feel like we're really there! We install speaker systems that could raise the dead (or our next-door neighbors), remote control devices to control everything that has an on/off switch, and cordless phones so we can always be multitasking. We have cars with DVDs, GPSs, and elaborate security systems to rival those in our houses.

And that's just the beginning. If we lack any of these things (or a numberless host of others), we feel somehow impoverished, like we aren't really full members of the real world.

A friend of mine told me about trying to explain to his twenty-three-year-old son that in a time of unemployment and relative poverty, it might not be wise to go in debt financing his sixty-dollar-a-month cell phone plan. The dad mildly suggested that it wasn't all that long ago that nobody had cell phones, and most of us seemed to survive just fine. That's where he lost the young man. His son simply couldn't conceive of life without a cell phone. You might as well ask him to survive a winter without shoes.

Let's put this in perspective. In the last half of the twentieth century, American society has gone from no televisions to one in every room. One home telephone on a party line has been replaced by omnipresent cell phones in every purse and on every belt clip. The convenience of electric typewriters with erasable paper was quickly upgraded to home computers—now with voice-recognition software!

There's just no question about it: We've never had so much stuff! In fact, our abundance has created the problem of relative poverty. People actually think of themselves as poor because they're not as well-off as a neighbor or friend or TV personality! And if they have to move backwards from a cable modem to dial-up service for the Internet, it's an affront to their sense of well-being.

While we operate with the myth that more money will bring us satisfaction, it doesn't. Although we are vastly wealthier than we have ever been in our history, the incidence of clinical depression has increased significantly in our culture. *And studies consistently show no notable relationship between personal wealth and personal satisfaction.* Wealth doesn't even show up on satisfaction's radar. Amazing! But no matter how many studies there may be, I don't think we really believe that—at least, not in *our* case. (If I won the lottery, I would be the one happy exception. Right!)

The apostle Paul warned his young friend, Timothy, about the deceit of riches: "For the love of money is a root of all kinds of evil, for which some have strayed from the faith in their greediness, and pierced themselves through with many sorrows" (1 Timothy 6:10).

In other words, these folks went hard after money to scratch that inner itch in their lives. But instead of finding satisfaction—to their amazement—they found wounds and pain beyond adequate description. The New Testament word used for "pierced" literally means "put on a spit." It conjures up a terrible picture of being pierced through and then roasted alive. Not my idea of a satisfying life!

In the book of Proverbs, a man named Agur wrote these words in his prayer journal: "Give me neither poverty nor riches; feed me with the food that is needful for me, lest I be full and deny you and say, 'Who is the LORD?' or lest I be poor and steal and profane the name of my God" (Proverbs 30:8–9, ESV).

IF ONLY...

Some people live their whole lives in the land of "If Only."

You may not find the coordinates on MapQuest or be able to put your finger on it in a world atlas. Even so, it seems to be the destination resort for untold multitudes looking for a little satisfaction in life. Chances are, you've visited this wistful, unhappy place a few times yourself.

If only I just looked different...

One glance in the mirror and the thought rushes back: *If only I were more beautiful.* Or handsome and studly. But what does that really mean? Do we need to be taller, maybe? Or in the case of some girls...shorter? Does it entail being more muscular, more curvy? Should we have darker hair, more hair, whiter teeth? Whatever it takes, Americans endure the risk, pain, and expense of the lifts, tucks, dyes, transplants, and tans in the belief that the payoff is worth it. ("Satisfaction guaranteed!")

Believe it or not, they line up for injections of botulism virus in the forehead, convinced that the temporary paralysis of those delicate facial nerves gives an unwrinkled, youthful appearance. But when they're pushing seventy, is anybody honestly going to think they're still thirty-nine?

If only I were thinner...

The $50 billion weight-loss industry keeps reminding Americans that they, too, can shed those unsightly pounds before swimsuit season opens! While it's true that as a nation we are obese and could stand to tone up, we also run the risk of being fixated on diets and dieting. That's what accounts for the struggles with bulimia and anorexia, which have led to way too many sad and untimely deaths. Underneath it all is the sense that if only we looked different, then we'd be satisfied. The truth? We'd be thinner, perhaps, but satisfied? Not likely.

If only I could just feel good...

That certainly sounds reasonable. Physical pain and chronic illness really take a toll on satisfaction as well. *It would be wonderful just to feel good for once!* But the football knee or the out-of-whack back or the anemia from the chemotherapy or the pesky migraines have a way of taking the fun out of life.

Unless you've been there, it's easy to underestimate how much pain wears on the psyche. I had one of those up-close-and-personal encounters with nagging pain myself after I recently fell and broke my shoulder. For months the aching and awkward sleep positions awakened me numerous times each night. As a result, I never felt rested in the morning, regardless of how many hours I'd logged between the sheets. Physical therapy three times a week for eight months with assigned "homework" was time-consuming drudgery. But I can tell you this: It allowed me to understand from the inside what somebody with chronic pain and weakness has to contend with.

It would be wonderful just to feel good for once! That's the same kind of wishful thinking that underlies reliance on alcohol or illegal drugs. Be it as a means to deal with pressure, a release valve for stress (or just the strain of life in general), some feel that if they could just ease the pain a bit, life would work better for them.

It usually begins rather benignly with, say, a drink after work with friends. But sooner than they might think, one drink has a way of taking on a life of its own, ultimately controlling their every move. *I'm not really an alcoholic*, they reason to themselves. *I can quit whenever I desire.* Really? So why don't they?

Methamphetamine is the current drug of choice. Talk about devastating! People steal, put their kids at risk, and generally do whatever they need to in order to score more. The psychological hit of meth is apparently so powerful people feel invincible, like they can work or play for days on end, needing no sleep at all. So they do. The problem is it's all a fantasy. The drug lies to them, all the while luring them to their own destruction—yet giving them *good feelings* along the way. So where does it end up?

One police officer in Oregon has made it a personal hobby to publish pictures of meth users as they have been photographed in repeated arrests. The first picture of one young woman was that of an attractive, full-of-life individual with her whole future ahead of her. A couple of years later in her next arrest photo she looked like she had aged at least twenty-five years, with facial skin looking like she'd been hit with buckshot![1]

So did meth satisfy her needs?

Only if she wanted to have rotting teeth, disintegrating internal organs, and the potential of infertility!

THE LIST GOES ON

The list of things people pursue to find satisfaction grows longer and more varied, depending on who is searching. Success, fame, security, intimacy or a host of other options appear attractive, but in the end, they all promise what they can't produce. People give their lives to chasing these objectives, yet they never find what they seek. To quote that aging rocker Mick Jagger they "can't get no satisfaction." In fact, they become increasingly dissatisfied.

Is it possible our own bodies hold clues for answering this? Consider the human body and how it functions in daily life. You eat, but regardless of how delicious or plentiful the food, you always get hungry again. You drink your favorite beverage; it's tasty and satisfying like always, yet you still get thirsty again. The same thing is true for your sexual relationship with your spouse. As exciting and beautiful as that experience might be, the feeling that accompanies the encounter simply doesn't last. Why is that?

In reality, the "satisfied" feelings accompanying all these basic functions of life *are intentionally designed to be transient.* Simply stated, if the actions weren't repeated, life would not continue. If we didn't eat, we'd die of starvation. If we didn't drink, we'd expire of dehydration. If we didn't reproduce, the human race would cease to exist. So in order to encourage life, the Creator built the same imperative into these three basic physical functions…the need to go after more!

Here's where things get really interesting. Although the usual, presumed sources of satisfaction aren't able to deliver the goods, there is a satisfaction that endures.

Over and over again, the Bible guarantees it.

It's found in the spiritual realm of our lives. Just as God wired us to need food, water, and sex, He has woven into the fabric of life itself a drive for meaning, fulfillment, and happiness.

It never goes away.

It can never be quenched or satiated by *anything* else.

Pascal called it a "God-shaped vacuum." And it has everything to do with the cultivation of a life that looks like Christ.

THE SECRET OF SATISFACTION

So…does this mean that all Christians experience a satisfaction denied to their nonbelieving neighbors?

Not at all.

Curiously enough, Christians often experience the same dissatisfaction as those who have no relationship with God at all. Though they apparently love God and know their sins are forgiven, they fail to understand that the *something* they are looking for has everything to do with Him. Built into our DNA is a longing for a relationship—a living, breathing, walking, talking friendship—with the Creator.

In the Sermon on the Mount, Jesus expressed this foundational truth this way: "Blessed are those who hunger and thirst for righteousness, for they shall be satisfied" (Matthew 5:6, ESV).

"Shall be satisfied…"?

Sounds like a guarantee to me.

Ponder this for a moment: We find the satisfaction we seek as we go after God, cultivating lives like His. Spiritual reality is more "real" than physical reality, which in the grand sweep of things is oh so fleeting.

Having more money, beauty, and physical strength cannot satisfy long term. God has so constructed us that the more we have lives with qualities reflecting Him and His character, the more we experience the happiness and enjoyment in life that we long for.

LOOK AT THE LIFE OF JESUS

There is no place we can see this reality expressed more fully than in the life of Jesus. When Jesus walked the earth as a man He experienced everything we all long for. No matter which character quality you consider, He embodied it. Nobody was more faithful than Jesus. Nobody was more forgiving, joyful, loving, patient, or obedient.

For that matter, His life expressed these qualities *completely*. This is a key reason He is so universally admired, why the crowds flocked to Him as He walked among them, and why people continue to be drawn to Him today—all over the globe, by the millions.

When you see how faithful He was, and what a dramatic impact that made on life after life, it inspires you to want to be more faithful yourself. His forgiving nature is beyond imagination, yet as you see what it accomplishes, you want to develop the same thing. When you get right down to it, Jesus embodies the satisfaction everybody desires deep within. If only we could exhibit a fraction of His godly character!

Well…as we give ourselves to the lifelong pursuit of those qualities that defined His life, we can.

Guaranteed.

IT'S A PROCESS

When we investigate this truth in the Bible, we learn that the satisfaction we seek is a *process*, not a *product*.

It's not a thing; it's an action.

It's not a destination; it's a journey.

We find the fulfillment, happiness, and meaning that we ache for in the process of hungering and thirsting for righteousness, for godly lives.

It's really true. It really works. God says so. And He has so fashioned us that as we cultivate His character in our lives and experience those rich and gratifying rewards...we find ourselves wanting more.

And more and more and more.

Jesus said as much in Mark 4:25: "For whoever has, to him more will be given." For example, the more forgiving we are, the healthier our lives will be. Our blood pressure, immune system, and relationships with others will be so enhanced we will want to be even more forgiving.

The same holds true for being thankful, content, patient, or any of the other matchless character qualities of Jesus. God uses these very qualities in our lives to draw us closer to Him and to reveal Himself to a world that doesn't recognize or know Him. The more our lives look like His, the more positive influence we have on all those around us, the better we feel about ourselves. And on it goes.

The secret of satisfaction? *Cultivating the character qualities of Christ.*

WIMPS NEED NOT APPLY

If you've never approached building character from this perspective, chances are it has seemed an almost insurmountable task. For most of us, developing godly character is a bit like dieting, where we pit psychology against physiology. While our mind says, *I'm going to lose that extra twenty pounds*, our body says, *Wanna bet?* And the battle begins.

So it is with character. We pit the flesh against the spirit, the reality of our fleshly selves against the desires of our spiritual selves. Again and again we fail. How many times have we said, *I'm going to be more patient*, only to turn around and snap at the next person we speak to? Determined as we might be, with an accountability partner and resolution to try harder/do better, we repeatedly take one step forward and two back.

How refreshing to come to the realization that the development of godly character is energized and motivated by God Himself! That's what the built-in rewards are all about. For example, as we begin the process of cultivating thankfulness, the feedback we get is so positive, the feelings we experience are so uplifting, it makes us want to do it all the more. And it's the same for other godly characteristics. Instead of feeling *driven* and forced to develop godly character, we are *drawn* by the Lord Himself to do so.

A quick review of the history of God's people demonstrates that the law only shapes behavior short term, whereas love shapes commitment for a lifetime. That's true of the development of character as well. The more consumed we are in cultivating godly character, the more exciting, fulfilling, vibrant, and meaningful our lives become.

The result? We are drawn by God Himself to continue the process.

WHERE FROM HERE?

With all this in mind, what are these qualities of character that bring us satisfaction? How do we encourage their development and stay on target? In the chapters that follow we will explore eleven different godly character qualities. We will define them, see how they have worked or are working in people's lives, recognize what happens when they are missing, find the payoffs that God builds into the development and expression of each one, and learn how to nurture their growth in our lives. We will also be given a test we can take that will help us evaluate how we're doing in that process, a gauge to measure our growth.

Before doing that, let's touch on an issue that affects us all. When we study character qualities, we quickly come face-to-face with our own imperfections and inadequacies. We have done things we wish had never taken place. Even though we are truly sorry, we feel disqualified. The tarnish will never be completely removed from our lives. Sadly, we can't undo the abortion, reunite the marriage, or return to our children's childhood and parent more lovingly and effectively. We can't erase that criminal record. So what's the point of pretending that we can be what we can't?

Because this study is all about God, and *what He can and will do with hearts that are focused on growing in His character.*

Never forget it—God is the God of the fresh start. Although Adam and Eve sinned in the Garden, God made them clothes and beckoned them into a new life. King David multiplied his transgressions and covered up adultery with murder, but he confessed his sin, and God continued to use him. The God of the second chance still fulfilled His promises to David. It's true that Peter denied the Lord to His face, yet Jesus forgave him, filled him with His Spirit, and used him to do incredible things in the early church.

So it is with you and me. If we confess our sin, God is faithful and just to forgive us and to cleanse us from all unrighteousness. (Guaranteed! See 1 John 1:9.)

We get to start fresh with Him.

We get to drive a stake and say with the apostle Paul, "But one thing I do, forgetting those things which are behind and reaching forward to those things which are ahead, I press toward the goal for the prize of the upward call of God in Christ Jesus" (Philippians 3:13-14).

From this point on, we can build lives that bear more and more resemblance to His. We can bring honor to the Lord and find rich rewards in the journey.

Everybody gets thirsty…and God has given us cool water and orange juice and iced tea and frosty mugs of root beer and all manner of wonderful thirst quenchers.

And in a way every bit as basic and elemental as thirst, everybody wants to be satisfied. God gives us both the secret and the means to find true satisfaction.

Dive into the process headfirst and put heaven's satisfaction guarantee to the test!

You don't have to remember an 800 number or have your Visa or MasterCard ready.

True satisfaction is both beyond price and absolutely free.

◆ POINTS TO PONDER ◆

1. Do you consider yourself satisfied? If so, why? If not, why not?

2. What roads have you traveled trying to find satisfaction? What routes did you think would get you there?

3. Describe the way in which a couple of people you know are searching for satisfaction right now.

4. Reflect on the idea that dissatisfaction may exist for a good reason.

5. What is the secret of satisfaction?

6. Explain the difference between satisfaction as a *product* and a *process.* Can you see how a sense of satisfaction develops in the process of building and expressing godly character qualities?

7. When He was here physically, did Jesus appear to be satisfied?

8. Are you feeling *driven* or *drawn* to express godly character qualities? What's the difference?

9. Do you believe that God will reward you as you cultivate His character in your life? How will those rewards look?

10. What if you feel like you've already blown it? Is there any point in pursuing godly character?

Chapter Two

What kills a skunk is the publicity it gives itself.

ABRAHAM LINCOLN

A man's pride will bring him low,
but the humble in spirit will retain honor.

PROVERBS 29:23

I t was one of *those* situations—so embarrassing you wish you could fade right out of the scene. At the same time, you're silently rejoicing and blessing heaven that it's not you!

But the truth is…the guy had it coming.

He was a "Somebody" with a capital "S." A major player and a minor celebrity in a small market (always the worst combination). He was one of those go-to guys everybody wants to have his picture taken with.

The situation in which he found himself on this particular day was so familiar he didn't even stop to look around and think it through. He could have walked through the whole drill blindfolded.

It was a wedding. He was a guest. Lots of people were there, and now it was time to be seated for dinner. Where else would a VIP like himself go but right up front? That's where he *always* sat.

He made his way through the crowd to the head table, smiling indulgently and shaking an occasional hand. Sure enough, there was an empty chair right next to the host's, so he took a seat, adjusting the table setting and sipping his water. He was on autopilot. Cruise control. He'd done this at hundreds of gatherings. The next thing was to greet the guests seated around him. He had just begun to chat with the attractive blonde next to him, completely oblivious to the fact that the host of the party was walking in his direction, accompanied by another guest.

Accustomed to the spotlight, he found himself in it yet again. But this time it didn't feel quite so gratifying. Every eye in the room locked onto the unfolding drama at the head table. Speaking in hushed tones and shaking his head, the host was clearly pointing to the back of the room. The seated man was in the wrong place. He'd need to get up and move. Now. He was sitting in a spot reserved for somebody else.

Move? In front of everybody?

Publicly humiliated, the man rose to his feet, excused himself, and began to slink to another table. He wanted to bolt out of the room and not look back, but felt like he was walking in ankle-deep mud. Sensing heads turning as he sought the folding chair in the back of the pavilion, he could only ask himself, *What was that? What in the world happened to me?*

Jesus told that story one day to a group of people who could easily relate. They had been invited to a dinner, and as they arrived everybody wanted the best, most prestigious place at the table. Everybody wanted to be noticed. Everybody wanted to be acknowledged and shown respect. And nobody but nobody wanted to be in a lesser place.

What Jesus discerned in their actions was a heart problem that—if left unchecked—would spread and taint every part of their lives. Wanting to save them from themselves and point them to a better way, He told that little story. Then came the clincher, the simple yet profound principle that applied to that generation and every one since: "For whoever exalts himself will be humbled, and he who humbles himself will be exalted" (Luke: 14:11).

Okay, let's be honest. "Humility" isn't a normal topic of conversation. We don't devote a lot of time to thinking about how it applies to our lives. And when we do, it's problematic because of our competitive American culture. How do you get to the top if you fight for the bottom? Does being humble equate to being a doormat? Whether it's your home, business, or athletic team, how do you succeed if you don't put yourself forward?

Bottom line: Is humility a realistic option in modern society?

According to Jesus' definition, humility is the one and only road to the success we seek. Humility is the recognition that God is God and we aren't. It's keeping our lives in proper perspective, not thinking of ourselves more highly than we ought to (or more lowly, for that matter). In a classic paraphrase of Romans 12:3–4, the J. B. Phillips version states: "Don't cherish exaggerated ideas of yourself or your importance, but try to have a sane estimate of your capabilities by the light of the faith God has given to you all."

While recognizing our value, abilities, and strengths, we use them to bring glory to God and a better life to those around us, instead of simply putting them into service for ourselves.

That's the key.

That's also the rub.

Humility recognizes that it's not about us!

HUMILITY SEES ITSELF WARTS AND ALL

The truly humble person views himself realistically. He doesn't perceive himself as being greater than he is, with talents and skills he doesn't possess. Neither does he overlook his strengths. He understands both his assets and his weaknesses and lives his life with both in full view. When it comes to his strengths and abilities, however, he politely refuses to take credit for them. He recognizes them as gifts to be treasured and invested in God's work.

With all of the powerful business, entertainment, and sports icons in contemporary culture, it's easy to forget about the figures that irrevocably changed history centuries ago. One such power person was a man named Moses.

No question that Moses was a can-do kind of guy. Is there any other way to characterize a man who began a new career at eighty, who freed over a million people from captivity without a single shot fired, and led them to be established in an entirely new country?

The ancient adventure began as the one-time shepherd went toe-to-toe with the pharaoh of Egypt, the superpower of his day. He proceeded to lead his people for forty years in the face of constant carping, grumbling, and Monday-morning quarterbacking. He fought off coup attempts and direct challenges to his leadership by jealous siblings and self-serving detractors. Not a bad résumé.

Yet look at God's assessment of this man: "Now the man Moses was very humble, more than all men who were on the face of the earth" (Numbers 12:3). With Moses' obvious strengths—a will of steel and the ability to withstand repeated attacks—why would God characterize him as *humble*?

Because Moses had a realistic appraisal of himself.

He must have known his strengths or he never would have taken on the task of leading God's people. Yet we read in Exodus 3 how well-aware he was of his weaknesses. If anything, he was so aware of his shortcomings he tried to talk God out of using him in the first place! Clearly God liked the fact that Moses saw himself "warts and all." God could do a lot with a man or woman like that.

He still can.

Have you ever noticed that *humility* and *CEO* usually don't appear in the same sentence? When the media highlights chief executives of significant companies, they describe a Big Dog, a rough-and-tumble player who has clawed his way to the top and enjoys all the perks of being there. While other mere mortals carry out the grunt work, he takes all the bows and photo ops that befit a man of his stature.

Curiously enough, companies run by executives fitting that description are rarely successful long term. Quite the reverse. Companies that prosper, that do far better than their peers, are often run by people who are very aware of their feet of clay, men and women who are hardly household names.

Take the case of Darwin Smith, the CEO who took Kimberly-Clark to a level it had never known. His ascension to leadership of the company was not exactly the stuff of novels. A somewhat reserved in-house attorney, Smith never seemed sure he had what it took to lead a great company. Years later when he was reflecting on why his leadership had helped the company become so strong, he said: "I never stopped trying to become qualified for the job."

Just two months after becoming CEO, Smith learned that he had a very aggressive form of nose and throat cancer, and was given less than a year to live. However…instead of going home and setting his house in order, he told the board that (a) he wasn't dead yet, and (b) he wasn't planning on checking out soon, so (c) he would keep doing what was needful until the time came that he couldn't.

As it happened, that time never came.[1]

Even throughout a trying treatment regimen, he still managed to do things men in perfect health only dream of accomplishing. And all the while, keenly aware of his strengths and weaknesses, he kept a low profile, shunning the spotlight and refusing to call attention to himself—organizing, inspiring, and leading Kimberly-Clark to become the leader in its field. That's what humility looks like.

HUMILITY ROLLS UP ITS SLEEVES
AND GOES TO WORK

A humble person doesn't wait for others to do the work; he digs right in and gets started. Leading by example, he sets an industrious pace by going the extra mile. Describing that humility in Jesus' life, Paul wrote, "Who, though he was in the form of God, did not count equality with God a thing to be grasped, but made himself nothing, taking the form of a servant, being born in the likeness of men. And being found in human form, he humbled himself by becoming obedient to the point of death, even death on a cross" (Philippians 2:6–8, ESV). Humility comes to serve, not to be served.

When our church began some thirty years ago, the attendance on the first Sunday was far more than we could have imagined. We had thought big, prayed hard, and hoped that if God was smiling on us we might have one hundred people.

Three hundred fifty showed up! But there was a flip side to that blessing. Along with all those people came expectations. With that many people, where were the ministries for children and youth? What about a choir?

Little did I know, those were the least of our challenges. The more difficult hurdle to clear each week was setup. Because we rented space in a high school and used the cafeteria for a sanctuary, we had to go in every Sunday, "tear down" the cafeteria, and set up folding chairs for the congregation. We brought in the stage, organ, sound system, and nursery furniture. The task was overwhelming! How could I pastor the people God was bringing and manage all the housekeeping duties besides?

That was when God sent Les.

With no fanfare, Les stepped forward and volunteered to handle all the setup. He organized teams of trailer-pullers who brought in our "church-in-a-box" each week. Other volunteers emptied the trailer and brought in the equipment while the third group disassembled the cafeteria.

Never before or since have I seen a better illustration of servanthood and humility at work! Even though Les was a successful businessman during the workweek, Sunday found him with shirtsleeves rolled up, slinging chairs every which way in the cafeteria. His work was so inspiring that it drew others to want to work with him. In a matter of a few weeks, we had seventy-five people involved in the setup ministry, and it was running like a Swiss watch.

Les never called attention to himself, even though he was always on the front lines leading the charge. You might say that he led the worship team, because the fellowship could not have gathered without the work that he oversaw. That's what humility looks like.

HUMILITY DOESN'T CARE WHO GETS THE CREDIT

A truly humble person isn't driven by the need to be front and center. Years ago T. A. Hill captured this truth musically in the song "Rhythm Guitar":

> Nobody wants to play rhythm guitar behind Jesus.
> It seems like everybody wants to be
> the lead singer in the band;
> I know it's hard to get a beat on what's divine,
> when everybody's pushin' toward the head of the line.

Some of the people who have made the greatest impact on the world around them are those who have stayed behind the curtain. They have been content with what they could accomplish for the greater good rather than keeping a tally of who-gets-credit-for-what.

One evening, shortly after she had won the Nobel Peace Prize for the work she had done among the poorest of the poor in India, Mother Teresa was interviewed by Johnny Carson on his popular television show. When Carson opined how difficult it must be to keep all that notoriety and fortune from going to her head, he was completely unprepared for her response.

Taking a moment to remind him of Jesus' famous ride into Jerusalem on a donkey on Palm Sunday with thousands upon thousands cheering Him on, she asked, "Do you think, Mr. Carson, for one moment, that that little donkey thought all the applause was for him?"

Johnny Carson, the king of the comeback, was speechless! Mother Teresa was simply describing her life. She, like the little donkey, did her work quietly, powerfully, consistently, but without need for fanfare. That's what humility looks like.

HUMILITY LIFTS UP OTHERS

Most everybody has heard of the apostle Paul, but few outside the faith are familiar with his partner Barnabas. Yet it was Barnabas who encouraged Paul and gave him the support he needed to accomplish what he did.

It was Barnabas who extended a hand of fellowship to the recently converted Saul of Tarsus, who later became "Paul." Saul's reputation for torturing and imprisoning Christians was widespread, and believers were reluctant to embrace him as a brother in Christ.

Not Barnabas.

He reached out to Saul when he arrived in Jerusalem and took him to meet both Peter and James, the heads of the church there.

Some years later, it was Barnabas who remembered Saul and traveled to Tarsus to invite him to join in leading the church in Antioch, an invitation Saul accepted gladly. Shortly thereafter the church launched the first missionary endeavor in history, and Barnabas and Saul were commissioned to make the trip, with Barnabas leading the team. By the end of their first major citywide effort in Paphos, however, Barnabas gladly took a second seat, and from that point on it was Paul and Barnabas—in that order.

Paul was in such poor health, however, that without Barnabas, he might well have perished before they reached the next city on their itinerary. Antioch of Pisidia was only accessible by climbing the treacherous Tarus mountain range, and Paul simply could not have survived without Barnabas' encouragement and support.

When the early church needed money to purchase food for the widows, it was Barnabas who quietly sold land he owned in Cyprus and gave all the proceeds to the church to use as it saw fit. The impact of that gift was immediate and remarkable, yet Barnabas didn't do it to gain notoriety. He did it to be supportive of the saints in Jerusalem. That's what humility looks like.

HUMILITY IS SEEN IN THE HEART

Jesus tells a great story about two men, one of whom was a proud Pharisee who constantly worked at burnishing his public image, and the other a detested tax collector. The Pharisee crowed loudly for all to hear: "God, I thank You that I am not like other men—extortioners, unjust, adulterers, or even as this tax collector. I fast twice a week; I give tithes of all that I possess."

Conversely, the tax collector stood off by himself and didn't even dare raise his eyes to heaven. While beating his breast as a sign of contrition, he prayed, "God, be merciful to me, a sinner!"

As Jesus summarized the story for His listeners, He noted that in God's eyes, the *tax collector* was the one on whom He smiled.

God is much more blessed by a humble heart than by self-righteous words and actions. We have all known people who have worked hard to give the appearance of humility, even when it was obvious they were *proud* of it! Humility isn't preoccupied with outward appearances; it's too caught up in bearing the fruit of humility.

THE HOW-TOS OF HUMILITY

"Working at humility" seems like an oxymoron. Yet the fact remains, if we are to weave this quality into the fabric of our lives, we need to have some sense of how that comes about. Following is a list of some things to be considered in the process of nurturing humility in your life:

- We recognize that God is God and we aren't. We are quick to give Him the glory for the good things that happen in our lives.
- We have an honest appraisal of ourselves, recognizing both our strengths and our weaknesses.
- We refuse to be self-centered, finding joy in serving those around us.
- We never see ourselves as being too good or too important for the tasks at hand.
- We are quick to give credit where credit is due, not seeking it ourselves.
- We are encouragers, affirming and building up others.
- We assume the best, refusing to suspect the worst.
- We're comfortable behind the scenes, not needing the spotlight.
- We accept responsibility for our shortcomings and failures, and learn from them.
- We accept the challenges God gives us, committing all we have and are to His service.

Certainly there are numerous other attitudes and approaches that will enhance the development of humility, but these are a good start.

And what benefits does God build into the character quality of humility? Certainly the list is long, but consider these:

A humble person…

> …is a happy person, loved by others.

> …leads a less stressful life than others, not feeling constrained to be who he isn't or do what he isn't equipped to do.

> …has peace in his life, knowing he doesn't have to live up to unrealistic expectations placed on him by himself or others.

> …rejoices in the success of others, creating positive relationships.

> …is optimistic, knowing that God is in charge of his life, capable of enabling him to accomplish any task before him.

> …enjoys his work, grateful he has a place to exercise his gifting.

Though it is a vanishing virtue in today's highly competitive culture, living a life of true humility makes a most powerful statement. William Penn said it so well years ago: "Sense shines with a double luster when it is set in humility. An able and yet humble man is a jewel worth a kingdom."

◆ POINTS TO PONDER ◆

1. Review the "how-tos of humility." How are you doing on each of these in your life currently? Which ones do you need the most work on?

2. Note specific steps you can take to improve expressing humility personally.

3. Which of the benefits of humility are you currently enjoying? Do you see the relationship between the "how-tos" and the benefits?

4. Think of a couple of people you know personally who express humility in their lives. Describe the specific ways they behave that lead you to regard them as humble.

5. Helen Keller once said, "I long to accomplish great and noble tasks, but it is my chief duty to accomplish humble tasks as though they were great and noble. The world is moved along, not only by the mighty shoves of its heroes, but also by the aggregate of the tiny pushes of each honest worker." What does she mean? How does it apply to your life?

TEST YOURSELF ON HUMILITY

PLEASE READ the following statements and ask yourself, **"Do I agree that this describes me—my thoughts and actions during the last few months?"** Then, CIRCLE a number on the scale (below) from 1 to 10, showing how strongly you disagree or agree that each statement does or does not apply to you. Thus, a "1" means that you totally disagree that this is a strength in your life and a "perfect 10" means that you totally agree that the statement describes one of your strengths.

Totally Disagree	Very Strongly Disagree	Strongly Disagree	Somewhat Disagree	Slightly Disagree	Slightly Agree	Somewhat Agree	Strongly Agree	Very Strongly Agree	Totally Agree
1	2	3	4	5	6	7	8	9	10

1. I often come close to being authentically humble.	1 2 3 4 5 6 7 8 9 10
2. God gives me strength to be humble and avoid arrogance.	1 2 3 4 5 6 7 8 9 10
3. I am humble around people outside the church.	1 2 3 4 5 6 7 8 9 10
4. I am a completely humble person.	1 2 3 4 5 6 7 8 9 10
5. I avoid thinking of myself more highly than I should.	1 2 3 4 5 6 7 8 9 10
6. I have given glory to God, not myself, for my successes.	1 2 3 4 5 6 7 8 9 10
TOTAL SCORE (Read directions) =	

SCORE YOURSELF ON HUMILITY

Take each of the numbered responses you circled, and add up the numbers to make a total score. For example, if you answered "7" to all 6

questions, the total would be 42. Write the total in the box below the questions, and also mark the location of your score on the chart below:

SCORING CHART FOR HUMILITY

(Mark a line through the location of your score)

6 10 15 20 25 30 35 36 37 38 39 40 41 42 43 44 45 46 47 48 49 50 51 52 53 54 55 56 57 60

INTERPRETING YOUR SCORE: The middle point (41) represents the average score obtained by typical readers. Below-average scores are 35 or less, and those below 25 are extremely low. Above-average scores are 49 or more, and scores above 56 are extremely high.

If your score is below average, discuss your results with a friend and see if you can identify possible areas of improvement in humility.

Chapter Three

Then Peter came to Him and said,
"Lord, how often shall my brother sin against me,
and I forgive him? Up to seven times?" Jesus said to him,
"I do not say to you, up to seven times,
but up to seventy times seven."

MATTHEW 18:21–22

Peter had probably given his question a lot of thought. He may have been trying to be more thoughtful, less impulsive. Undoubtedly he had rehearsed some conflicts and offenses he had experienced in his own life, and had arrived at a conclusion that he thought godly and generous.

Seven times.

Almost certainly he was pleased with himself. The traditional "religious" limit for extending forgiveness was three times, and he was more than doubling that. Seven times! Wasn't seven the perfect number? Nobody would expect a person to extend forgiveness to that degree. Jesus might even give him an "atta boy" for coming to such a gracious conclusion. Yessir, all that teaching was really sinking in.

But it wasn't to be. Jesus didn't respond at all like Peter thought He would (when did He ever?). The Lord's response made him blush. Instead of patting the big fisherman on the back and complimenting him on his show of mercy, Jesus replied: "I do not say to you, up to seven times, but up to seventy times seven."

In other words, God requires that forgiveness be *limitless*. As long as a person repents of his sin, forgiveness is required. Period.

What? Is that even possible?

NOTHING EASY ABOUT IT

As was true for Peter, so for people today: Forgiveness is one of the most difficult Christian character qualities to cultivate and express. It's probably no stretch to say that for most of us it is *the* most challenging character quality to develop. The burning question is: How do we do it?
Even mentioning the subject smacks you right in the face with *that* struggle, the one you've worked so hard to forget. It's been years, and still the emotions explode to the surface like the day it happened.

Your husband was going through a difficult time in his life. For reasons that ultimately proved to be medical, he was depressed, *really* depressed. In fact, he was so down that one day he confided in you he had even contemplated suicide.

Oh, he really wouldn't go there. You made him promise he wouldn't. Still, he wasn't doing well. It was such a hard thing to deal with, to keep inside, yet he knew if others found out it would do irreparable damage to his reputation. It could even cost him his job. That's why he was so thankful that he had you to confide in. You were there for him, and he knew it.

As the days went by, the burden of his struggle became so heavy that you shared it in confidence with your best friend. You did that because you knew she would never betray the trust you had in her. She never had before; why would she start now?

In your wildest dreams you never thought she would disclose it to anybody, *let alone to her prayer group at church.* So when another woman sidled up to you in the aisle at the grocery store and while furtively looking around, asked how Hal was doing with his depression, you almost fainted. As you quietly, frantically conversed with her and found out what she knew and where she got her information, your panic turned to rage. *How could anyone who called herself a friend do such a thing?* Why would she knowingly risk destroying Hal and you right along with him? Who did she think she was to treat the trust you placed in her with such utter disregard? How could you ever forgive her?

And what would happen when Hal found out? Surely he would find out, no doubt through a "caring" husband of one of the ladies in the prayer group. When he did, what would that do to his already fragile emotional state? How could he ever trust *you* again? How could he find it in his heart to forgive you? Just saying the word "forgiveness" brings it all rushing back into your mind. It almost makes you sick to your stomach to think about it!

So what do you do in a situation like that, especially when your emotions are running amuck? Suck it up, bury it deep down inside, and hope it will all go away? Organize your life in such a way that you will never see her again? Spew venom at the very mention of her name? How do you handle hurt?

LET IT GO

Before we tackle that question, let's understand exactly what "forgiveness" really means, and what's actually expected of us.

Contrary to popular opinion, the word most frequently used for forgiveness in the Bible doesn't mean to be a nice guy and act as though nothing is wrong when somebody does something hurtful to you. Neither does it mean you let bygones be bygones, nor act as though nothing horrible happened and then go fishing with the one that hurt you the next time he asks. When you get right down to it, forgiveness has a lot less to do with forgetting about a hurtful situation or maintaining a bad relationship than it does with dealing with the emotions that arise from the hurtful act itself.

At its base, forgiveness simply means to *let go* or *disregard*. When you forgive, you aren't letting go of the memory of the offense or the offender; rather, you're letting go of the emotional baggage you carry in your life as a result of their act(s). In that sense forgiveness has more to do with you than it does with the one who hurt you.

Undoubtedly that is why God makes it such a high priority in our lives. He knows that if we continue to bury the pain or carry the hurt in our hearts for offenses done to us, it will slowly but surely rob us of joy and peace.

That's why He tells us to forgive, to let go. When we choose to hang on to the pain of a transgression against us, it gnaws on our minds and hearts like a dog on a bone. But when we forgive, choosing to release the emotional turmoil and desire for retaliation or revenge that so often flare up after such an offense, we clear the deck of our lives for a fresh start.

Forgiveness is sheer mercy...*for us*. It has much more to do with God's grace and kindness in our lives than it does with the one who has committed the offense.

Contrary to what we sometimes think, when we say, "I forgive you," it's not a form of "all ye, all ye outs in free." We're not communicating that the phrase undoes the damage or consequences, either to us or the one who has hurt us. Instead, when we forgive, we disarm the power of the offense to trap us in our anger or focus our hearts on the pain. We intentionally refuse to dwell on our hurt, nurse our wounds, or rehearse our reasons for resentment. Rather than focusing on the assault and the assailant and exercising our "right" to be angry, we choose to let that emotional baggage go. And that simple (though oh-so-difficult) decision changes everything for the better.

ALL SIN IS AGAINST GOD

One clear truth that helps us get to this place in our lives is realizing that all sin is ultimately against God. Though we are the recipients of the specific transgression and have to deal with the pain it produces, the sin itself is against God.

King David understood this truth. In a particularly ugly incident in his life, though David wreaked havoc on two different lives, he knew his real sin was against God. That's why when he was finally faced with his transgressions he cried out to God, saying, "Against You and You only have I sinned." Yes, he had hurt two people. But on a profoundly deeper level, he had sinned against his Lord.

Precisely because the sin is against God, we need to realize that He is the One who will deal both with the sin and the sinner. In spite of what we might do or fantasize doing, nobody is going to get away with anything. That's the nature of sin. So even though superficially we are the ones who bear the brunt of the blows, it is God who experiences the greatest pain. And He will deal with the one who has inflicted it.

What are we saying here? We're saying that when the peace in our lives has been shattered by an unprovoked attack, and we know exactly who is responsible, instead of mulling over our counterattack, we need to choose to forgive. Knowing that God will do what needs to be done, we choose to extend forgiveness. We release the offender from the need to "make it right" with us by means of three exceedingly powerful words: *"I forgive you."*

We literally declare we are not going to be held hostage by our pain. We opt to let it go.

WASHING AWAY THE ACID

Funny…when you read these words, thinking about the process of forgiveness, it doesn't sound particularly difficult. In fact, it may sound
downright easy. After all, dwelling on difficulties never really helped
anybody, right? God's in control, so why not let Him fight those battles?

To move forgiveness from theory to reality in our lives, we need to
recognize that holding on to our hurts—although a natural response—
is both harmful to us and does nothing to resolve the situation. Actually
the consequences are far worse. The tragic biblical story of Ahithophel,
perhaps King David's closest friend, gives us the gory details.

During the bulk of David's career he and Ahithophel were inseparable.
Turn one around and you saw the other. Because Ahithophel had such
a unique ability to give wise, godly counsel, David depended heavily on
him. Certainly that is why one particular action of David's proved to be
so devastating to his faithful friend, and hurt him so deeply he lost all
perspective.

One of the most familiar stories in the Bible is that of David and
Bathsheba. Bathsheba was a young married woman who fell prey to
King David's unbridled lust. As a result of their encounter, when David
discovered that Bathsheba was pregnant, he panicked. Her husband
had been away from home for an extended period of time fighting a
war, so it would be readily apparent the child was not his own.

Frustrated and flustered, David quickly conspired with the com-
mander of his troops to have Bathsheba's husband killed in battle.
Because of the way the death occurred, nobody would be the wiser, and
with her husband out of the picture, David would have the opportunity
to take Bathsheba into his own house. How generous of him to reach
out and care for the widow of one of his fallen mighty men! How noble!
And so he did.

What David failed to consider was the fact that Bathsheba was not an orphan. She had an extended family that cared for her deeply, a family that was so close they kept tabs on her life. That family included a highly devoted grandfather. Ahithophel.

Can you imagine his anger when he put two and two together, when he determined what David had done to his granddaughter and her husband? Can you envision how hurt he would have been to think that his best friend would have done such a hideous thing, especially to his granddaughter?

Ahithophel was enraged! Filled with bitterness, all he could think of was revenge. Biding his time, looking for an opportune moment, Ahithophel was obsessed with finding a way to make David pay for what he had done.

What Ahithophel failed to realize was the fact that David's sin was against God, and that God was highly involved in the matter. The Lord knew all about David's sin, and had already determined how He would use this situation for purposes known only to Him. A quick death arranged by Ahithophel was not a part of His plan. Having to live through the death of two sons, flee his kingdom, and see his extended family humiliated publicly would prove to be more difficult for David to deal with than a swift thrust of the sword by his former friend.

By the time Ahithophel realized God was not with him, it was too late. He felt trapped, backed into a corner of his own making. Seeing no other way out, he followed the only course he felt was open to him: He took his own life. Though he had desired to destroy David, his bitterness drove him to destroy himself.

The moral of the tragic story of Ahithophel is that *bitter never makes better*. In numerous studies done by a variety of researchers on this subject, consistently they find a lack of forgiveness is a risk factor for cardiovascular disease, provides fertile soil for depression with all its attendant problems, tends to lower the functioning of the immune system, and increases the risk for some forms of cancer. Harboring hurt in your heart is deadly! Difficult as it may be to accept, it's as simple as this: If you want to experience a life of peace and joy, you must forgive.

But what is it going to take?

LOOK IN THE MIRROR

Before anything else, you need to look in the mirror (and read Matthew 18:15–17 while you're at it). It is essential to remember that you, too, stand in need of forgiveness both from God and other people.

Remember the old spiritual? "It's me, it's me, O Lord, *standin' in the need of prayer…*"

It should be easy to recall a time when you were swallowed up in embarrassment and humiliation due to your own bad decisions, and you yearned deeply to be forgiven, to have things made right.

Refresh your memory about pleading with God to forgive you and the gracious release from guilt and shame that washed over you as you experienced His forgiveness. What sweet freedom! This is exactly what you now have the opportunity to pass on. Remembering the experience of being forgiven is the first step to take in the process of forgiving others.

CLEAR THE AIR

The next step is to deal directly with the one who hurt you. Let's say you're a woman who has been hurt by another woman, a friend. Leaving your weapons behind, you need to confront her, preferably face-to-face, clarifying what she has done and how it has affected you. Strange as it may seem, she may not even be aware of the offense! It's possible she thought the action that tore you apart was going to help you.

It's critical to clear the air with the one who has caused the pain before any other steps are taken. That's where relationships are restored and hurts are healed. It's important not to involve others in this step, because it complicates matters for everybody. It can create bad feelings for those dragged into the difficulty, as well as draw an inaccurate picture of everybody concerned. So before anything else takes place, take the tough step of face-to-face—or at the very least phone-to-phone—confrontation.

GET A REFEREE

The whole troubling episode might end right there, with the difficult but cleansing process of clearing the air.

But what if it doesn't?

If the individual either refuses to take responsibility for what she has done, or gets defensive and lashes back, then there's more work to be done. The last thing you want to do is shrug your shoulders and walk away, because truth be known, you *won't* walk away. At least not in your heart!

If she refuses to listen or take responsibility, at that point the next step is to get somebody else involved who is willing to mediate, a neutral party who might be able to diffuse the emotion and facilitate resolution. Is it possible that you misunderstood the whole thing? Or could it be that your friend isn't seeing the whole picture, isn't understanding how deeply she has wounded you?

If the perpetrator is an active believer, it might be beneficial to involve her pastor. If the two of you belong to different churches, you both might feel more comfortable if each of your pastors participated. However that works, your main desire needs to be closure. Will your relationship ever be exactly as it was before the offense took place? Perhaps not. But that isn't the point. The point is that in the long term, everyone involved will learn, grow, and keep walking with God.

CHOOSE THE HIGH GROUND

So what if you simply don't have the wherewithal to extend forgiveness? What if you find it impossible to say (honestly), "I forgive you"? When you boil it all down, there are really only two options.

On the one hand you can choose to sit and stew in your own juices, allowing the acid of your bitterness to eat away at the lining of your joy. That's certainly your choice, though not a very wise one.

On the other hand you can reach out to God, asking Him to give you the strength you do not possess to do the right thing.

Knowing that it's God's desire that we forgive, isn't there really only one option? Isn't it better to let go before the emotional current sucks you into a whirlpool of destruction? God is in control, and He is at work. You need to learn from Ahithophel and not try to do God's work for Him. Let God be God and follow His plan.

They say a picture is worth a thousand words. Perhaps the most powerful picture of forgiveness you could lock onto is that of Jesus dying on the cross. As He was going through the agony of one of the most excruciatingly painful forms of death ever devised by the evil heart of man, He looked over the crowd. There were people jeering Him who had cheered Him just a couple of days before. Those who said, "Blessed is He who comes in the name of the Lord," now spit at Him and shouted, "He saved others. Let Him save Himself!"

How could they be so fickle? How could they mock Him in His misery? He had treated them with kindness and generosity, feeding, teaching, healing, and blessing them. Which of them had He ever hurt?

If anybody ever had cause to be bitter, it was Jesus. Yet what did He pray from the cross? *"Father, forgive them for they don't know what they're doing."* With or without repentance, He forgave. Though He had every right to be angry, instead He chose to let it go. His love for His attackers left no room for vengefulness.

Jesus looks for that same response in all those who truly follow Him. In Matthew 6, He says, "For if you forgive men their trespasses, your Heavenly Father will also forgive you. But if you do not forgive men their trespasses, neither will your Father forgive your trespasses" (v. 14–15). Because you have received forgiveness, you can express it to others; because you express forgiveness, you open yourself to experience it more and more.

And oh, what beautiful benefits...

THE BEAUTY OF THE BENEFITS

When you survey the vastness of the physical, emotional, and spiritual benefits of forgiveness, you have to wonder why anyone would choose *not* to forgive. Yes, you can make the decision to withhold forgiveness, living in the fantasy that you're "punishing" the offender.

In reality, the only one being punished is you.

Rarely does the perpetrator of the offense think about the one they've offended, and even more rarely do they obsess over what their "victims" may be thinking about them. So who really wins when you withhold forgiveness?

When you forgive, not only does the Bible present you with a myriad of accompanying blessings, but scientific research is quite conclusive as well. Whether you study the research done by the Stanford Forgiveness Project, the International Forgiveness Institute at the University of Wisconsin, or work by researchers like Dr. Michael McCullough, the positive benefits of forgiveness are overwhelming.

What sort of benefits? Less cardiovascular disease, lower blood pressure, a stronger immune system, higher self-esteem, lower rates of depression and anxiety, an increased sense of hope, a calmer life, and an increased ability to deal with day-to-day stress are just a few of the many wonderful rewards. When it clearly makes your life work better, why would anybody choose anything else?

Born out of love, obedience, and selflessness, there is no quality nearer to the heart of God than forgiveness. May the prayer Jesus taught His disciples be a basic prayer in your heart: "Forgive me for my sins as I forgive others for their sins against me."

Want your satisfaction guaranteed?

Then by all means *forgive!*

◆ POINTS TO PONDER ◆

1. With this chapter in mind, explain to somebody else what *forgiveness* means.

2. Describe how you feel when you forgive somebody (free, cheated, relieved, wary, hopeful...). Describe how you feel when somebody forgives you (free, vindicated, humble, guilty, released...).

3. Identify a past situation when you were offended or hurt. How did you express forgiveness? What steps did you take? How could you have handled it more effectively? Use the same process with a current situation. What will a resolution require?

4. How can you tell if you have truly forgiven somebody?

   Do you rehearse the specifics of the incident repeatedly, yet insist it doesn't bother you anymore?

   Do you still have strong emotions when you think of the situation?

   Do you believe God has dealt with or is dealing with the other person?

   Are you obsessed with discovering whether the other person has changed?

   Do you find that you think about it less and less with decreasing emotion?

Do you feel on edge or relaxed when you see the person?

Can you pray positively for the one who hurt you?

5. Think of yourself standing before God accounting for the last few sins you have committed.

   What would you desire God to do for you?

   Would you want Him to express mercy and grace?

   Would you want Him to keep rehearsing your failure, pointing out how far you missed the mark?

   Would you desire more to experience His love and compassion, and know that you are in fellowship with Him again?

   What are the implications of this for an offense a friend has committed against you?

   Do you understand the relationship between being forgiven and forgiving?

TEST YOURSELF ON FORGIVING

Please read the following statements and ask yourself, "**Do I agree that this describes me—my attitudes and actions during the last few months?**" CIRCLE a response number on the scale from 1 to 6, showing how strongly you disagree or agree that each statement does or does not apply to you.

Very Strongly Disagree	Somewhat Disagree	Slightly Disagree	Slightly Agree	Somewhat Agree	Very Strongly Agree
1	2	3	4	5	6

1. I often forgive people for things that have hurt me.	1 2 3 4 5 6
2. God gives me strength to forgive difficult people.	1 2 3 4 5 6
3. I can consistently forgive people who wrong me.	1 2 3 4 5 6
4. I have truly forgiven myself for past mistakes.	1 2 3 4 5 6
5. I strive to make my heart as forgiving as possible.	1 2 3 4 5 6
6. People can see that I show forgiveness.	1 2 3 4 5 6
7. I have restored friendships by forgiving those who hurt me	1 2 3 4 5 6
TOTAL SCORE (Read directions) =	

SCORE YOURSELF

Take each of the numbered responses you circled, and add up the numbers to make a total score. For example, if you answered "4" to all 7

questions, the total would be 28. Write the total in the box below the questions, and also mark the location of your score on the chart below:

SCORING CHART FOR FORGIVENESS

(Mark a line through the location of your score)

7.......**15**....20....**25**....30 31 32 **33** 34 35 36 **37** 38 39 **40** 41 42
———

INTERPRETING YOUR SCORE: The middle point (33) represents the average score obtained by typical readers. Below-average scores are 25 or less, and those below 15 are extremely low. Above-average scores are 37 or more, and scores above 40 are extremely high.

If your score is below average, discuss your results with a friend and see if you can identify possible areas of improvement in forgiving others.

Chapter Four

Some people are always grumbling that roses have thorns;
I am thankful that thorns have roses.

ALPHONSE KARR

The worst moment for the atheist is when
he is really thankful and has nobody to thank.

DANTE ROSSETTI

Back in the early seventies, a spunky lady named Frances Gardner Hunter wrote a book entitled *Praise the Lord Anyway*. The humble little paperback detailed how Mrs. Hunter had learned the benefits of expressing gratitude to God no matter what was going on in her life.

The book became a bestseller, ultimately gaining her an opportunity to speak before a large crowd at the Christian Booksellers Association annual convention. Thrilled at the opportunity to address this group, the lady went all-out in preparation. Leaving nothing to chance, she selected just the right dress, made certain her makeup and hair looked terrific, and took her seat in the large convention hall.

The long-anticipated moment finally arrived. Frances Hunter was introduced and, accompanied by enthusiastic applause, made her way to the podium.

If you've ever stood before an audience to speak, you're probably aware that your mind works on several levels simultaneously. While one part of you remembers to smile, gesture appropriately, and begin your address, another part of your consciousness notes details of your surroundings—the lights, the audience, the sound system, and maybe a fussy child in the back of the room.

It was the same with Mrs. Hunter. As she began to speak, she noted that the stage did not seem especially solid. It was almost as though it had a bit of give. Brushing aside such distracting thoughts, she continued her hilarious presentation of praising the Lord in all circumstances.

Midway through her talk, however, the stage suddenly became the all-important issue. She felt it slowly collapsing in front of her. Before she could respond, she began sliding forward. In the process, the boom holding the microphone hooked her hair, which happened to be a wig. While Frances kept sliding, her lovely hairdo was now turned totally sideways. Finally her legs went out from under her and she rather force-fully sat down, and slid onto the convention floor!

Everyone sat in shocked silence and waited for what would happen next.

The speaker stood up, straightened her dress, shook her head, flashed a huge smile, and said, "Well, praise the Lord anyway!"

From that moment on, no one had any doubt that this lady practiced what she preached! Shaken and disheveled as she was, she presented a compelling picture of optimism and trust in the face of calamitous circumstances.[1]

Praise the Lord anyway?

A couple of millennia before Mrs. Hunter wrote her little book, the apostle Paul penned a slim little volume of his own. Paul's book was called First Thessalonians, and it too had practical advice for believers when things don't turn out precisely according to plan.

THANKFULNESS: STRANGE ADVICE?

When Paul arrived at Thessalonica and began the process of planting a church and discipling new believers, he had no concept he'd be given the left foot of fellowship by the townspeople after just a few weeks.

In fact, his antagonists were so vocal and strident that he had to slip out of town rather quickly, under cover of night. How distressing that must have been for a missionary with a big shepherd's heart! His hasty departure meant leaving his fledgling fellowship on its own to survive against formidable odds. If his adversaries were as difficult as they had been when he was present, what would they be able to do to people who were so young in their Christian faith? Could this little church persevere?

As it turned out, the Thessalonians not only survived, they thrived! Standing strong and true against the odds, they held out the bright banner of new life in Jesus Christ in a city where His name was all but unknown. In spite of the hostile environment, their church grew in numbers, with new converts even reaching out to other cities to declare the gospel. Amazing!

Given Paul's lack of time to build a solid foundation for the church, however, a few serious questions needed to be answered. So the apostle wrote them a letter to complete the instruction he'd been unable to deliver in person.

As the battered missionary neared the close of his letter, however, he made a most curious remark...that may have inspired an author named Frances Hunter in the distant future: "Rejoice always, pray without ceasing, in everything give thanks; for this is the will of God in Christ Jesus for you" (1 Thessalonians 5:16–18).

The "pray without ceasing" part certainly made good sense. This little band of beleaguered believers needed all the help it could get, especially from above. But...was it truly God's will that they rejoice *always* and give thanks in *everything*, especially given the challenges they faced? How could they do that? And more basically, why should they?

THANKFULNESS CHANGES EVERYTHING

Though the people may not have understood the full significance of Paul's exhortation at the time, he was giving them life-changing words of wisdom. The more thanks they expressed, the more they would remember God's love for them and His presence with them. Gratitude to God for all the marvelous things He had done, was doing, and had planned for their future would enable them to see obstacles and frustrations transformed into possibilities and hope.

As the believers in that hostile city confronted powerful opposition to their newfound faith, Paul wanted to equip them to experience happiness and a sense of well-being in the process.

To do that, they needed to approach life thankfully.

It was the only way. In fact, it still is.

Thankfulness for the people in the church at Thessalonica was a matter of focus. The Lord didn't expect them to gush gooey gratitude for their opponents' dirty tricks, the name-calling, the raw intimidation, and the underhanded attempts to smear and discredit. Even so, they could thank God...

...for the many good things in their lives.

...for the endless new things they were learning about their heavenly Father and His Kingdom.

...for each fresh new day to be alive and at work for Him.

...for minds capable of discerning His leading.

...for doors opening to the gospel, in their city and beyond.

They could certainly thank God for His character, His kindness, and His love, as He promised through the prophet Jeremiah: "For I know the plans I have for you...plans for wholeness and not for evil, to give you a future and a hope" (Jeremiah 29:11, ESV).

These believers could choose to see their cup as half empty, or instead use this as an opportunity to see God fill it to overflowing!

THANKFULNESS PAYS HUGE DIVIDENDS

When we take a good look at thankfulness, we find (once again) that God has built astounding benefits into this quality itself.

Over the last several years there has been considerable research by a variety of people on the subject of gratitude. The results have revealed—quite apart from the spiritual benefits—that amazing perks accrue to the one who approaches life gratefully.

One of the preeminent researchers in this field, Dr. Robert Emmons, says that: "Gratitude research is beginning to suggest that feelings of thankfulness have tremendous positive value in helping people cope with daily problems, especially stress, and to achieve a positive sense of the self."[2]

And that's just the beginning of the bounty. The tip of the proverbial iceberg.

People who feel grateful (to others, God, or even to creation in general) are generally more optimistic, have higher vitality, suffer less stress, and experience less clinical depression than the general population. This finding is true regardless of age, health, or income! Further, these people don't place as much value on *stuff* or *status* to make them happy, so they rate themselves much more frequently as satisfied.[3]

In a study conducted with college students, those who kept a weekly journal of things to be grateful for were found to exercise more regularly, have fewer physical problems, and feel better and more optimistic about their lives as a whole than those who chronicled only the negative or neutral parts of their lives. The students who recorded their gratitude also made greater progress toward meeting personal goals.

When the students ramped up their recording from weekly to daily—a form of "counting their blessings" every day—they were found to have higher levels of alertness, enthusiasm, determination, attentiveness, and energy than those who did not approach their lives in the same way. They found themselves more likely to help others enduring seasons of struggles in their lives.[4]

Even those with neuromuscular disease discovered that when they concentrated on the things they had to be grateful for, they had greater amounts of high energy, positive moods, and optimism. They slept better both in terms of quality and duration than did their counterparts who approached life without thinking about gratitude.[5]

Another gratitude researcher, Dr. Michael McCullough, has determined that grateful people are happier, more generous and forgiving, less envious and materialistic, and more religious or spiritual in general. "Grateful people seem to be focused on savoring the good things that they have already received in life, and may simply feel that they do not have time to concern themselves with resenting other people for what they have," he states.[6]

Studies have shown that consistently thankful people tend to get involved in more altruistic things like volunteering, tutoring, and giving financially to worthy causes. As if that weren't enough, it also appears as though grateful men and women live longer!

This current research substantiates biblical statements like these:

A merry heart makes a cheerful countenance, but by sorrow of the heart the spirit is broken. (Proverbs 15:13)

All the days of the afflicted are evil, but he who is of a merry heart has a continual feast. (Proverbs 15:15)

A merry heart does good, like medicine, but a broken spirit dries the bones. (Proverbs 17:22)

Long before researchers set out to evaluate the salutary effects of gratitude, God encouraged His people to develop it, commit to it, maintain it, and live in it. He knew that it was invaluable—because (surprise!) He *designed* it that way.

CONSIDER THE ALTERNATIVE

Being thankful makes even more sense when you consider the alternative. Who likes to be around grumpy, whiney, and cynical people? One well-known author poignantly states that it was primarily her own bitterness and resentment that caused the dissolution of a fourteen-year relationship. Evidently she found it so easy to focus on what needed to be changed, fixed, or updated, that she had little space left to celebrate what was right and good.

We've all known people with a penchant for seeing the dark side of everything. If there is a negative way to look at reality, they're all over it. For those doom-and-gloom merchants, the cup isn't even half empty; it's been shot full of holes! Is it any wonder that their lives aren't fun—or that people don't choose their company? Dark pessimism might be cute in a donkey named Eeyore, but in real life it doesn't wear very well.

Is it surprising that these negative folks are more anxious, prone to experience more stress? How could it be otherwise?

Marriages that focus on differences, that magnify and continually reexamine problems, are bumpy at best. While it's impossible to find the perfect relationship, marriages that major on the negatives and minor on the positives are destined for the counselor's office. That is, if they don't go directly to court!

The same dynamic proves true in the parent-child realm as well. Of course it does! How could it be otherwise? When parents continually chip away at their children, even for "necessary" correction, they will ultimately find they have little relationship with their kids at all.

Consider the difference that a grateful attitude makes. When couples are continually thankful for one another and for the opportunity they have to build a future together, the sky is the limit in their relationship. When children are regarded as a gift from God instead of a burden to be tolerated, they, too, will develop grateful hearts and express appreciation for their own lives. In all ways it just makes good sense to approach life thankfully.

So what does it take to cultivate thankfulness—especially if it doesn't seem to come naturally? What kinds of things can you do to help it develop in your life? Although the following suggestions may sound a bit elementary, they are bona fide means of expanding both the inward feeling of thankfulness and its outward expression. Just because ideas are simple it doesn't mean they are less true!

Sandwich Your Day with Thankfulness

The psalmist says it so well: "It is good to give thanks to the LORD, and to sing praises to Your name, O Most High; to declare Your lovingkindness in the morning, and Your faithfulness every night" (Psalm 92:1–2). There is something powerful about setting the pace for the day with a thankful heart. Whether you do this by journaling or prayer—or maybe a hearty praise chorus in the shower!—the same benefits accrue.

For Betty and me, one of the first things we do every day is pray together. And that usually begins with expressions of thanks.

No doubt our surroundings help.

As we sit at the breakfast table in rural western Washington State and look out the windows, we are greeted by more wildlife than seems fair for one couple to enjoy. Sometimes a great blue heron hunts for breakfast in one of our ponds, or geese and ducks paddle from one side to the other, or a coyote comes dancing across the meadow. Whatever it is, our spirits are lifted instantly.

Whether it's a fog-enshrouded day, so that the heron looks like an old man in a trench coat, or it's one of those crystal-clear blue-sky days when it seems like we could reach out and touch Mt. St. Helens or Mt. Hood, we can't help but say "thanks"—even when we've had our share of heartaches.

So that's how we begin every day of our married lives. Thankfulness is Job One.

Closing out the day with thanksgiving causes you to meditate on what is praiseworthy, as we are instructed in Philippians 4. In those last twilight moments of consciousness when you're drifting off to sleep, note one or two things for which you are thankful. It may be something as simple as the joy you experienced seeing the first daffodil of the season blooming in your flowerbed. Perhaps you remember a significant conversation with a coworker, or revisit the beaming smile on your daughter's face as she gave you the good news about her science project. Whatever it is, the appreciation that you savor will set the pace for a restful, peaceful night.

Could this be new territory for you?

If so, make a conscious commitment to try it for a couple of weeks. There is no question that once you begin, you'll keep going. The benefits just won't let you quit!

Be Thankful for the Little Things

When you think about it, most of life is comprised of little things. As you move through the course of your day, be thankful for the common graces and the minor miracles.

Giving sincere thanks before a meal illustrates my point. While the act may seem inconsequential, expressing thanks for the "basics" makes you more aware that the pieces of your life are a series of gifts.

As you do this, you will begin to recognize blessings that you previously took for granted. Somebody toiled to produce the crops that moved through the system to become the wonderful bread that gives you enjoyment and nourishment. How blessed we are to have such wonderful food! Appreciation for the little things has a way of adding up to an attitude of thanksgiving.

Keep a Thankfulness Journal

If there is anything researchers have nailed down, it's the value of journaling. Those who take the time and effort to note their reasons for gratitude are far better off for the process. Keeping a weekly journal is very helpful, but daily tabs are even better.

Don't discourage yourself by making the task more elaborate than necessary. Just take a few moments at the end of the day to jot down a list or a sentence about things for which you are grateful that day. The more you do it, by the way, the more you will notice. Your "gratitude quotient" will increase, and with it, physical stamina, optimism, and other seemingly unrelated blessings.

Find Reasons to Express Thanks...and Do It!

What would happen if you started to express gratitude in situations where it was neither demanded nor expected? Try doing it as an experiment for a couple of weeks. Challenge yourself to notice something new each day and thank the person who provided it.

Your shirts got ironed and "magically" appeared in your closet.

The lawn looks especially neat when it's freshly mown.

Somebody actually listened when you explained your whole crazy idea!

Whatever the specific, express appreciation five times a day for the next two weeks, even if it feels strange or forced when you begin. The fact is, the more you do it, the more positive feedback you will receive, and the more you will *want* to express thanks. As with the other steps listed here, this will only add to your attitude of gratitude, slowly but surely changing your worldview.

Praise the Lord Anyway!

Finally, regardless of what happens in the course of the day, be thankful. If the stage collapses beneath your feet, and the microphone twists your wig or toupee as you're en route to landing on your backside before a thousand watching eyes, thank God if it's only your dignity that gets injured. Join Frances Hunter with a smile that will scatter the forces of hell, and "praise the Lord anyway."

No, you didn't ask for the flu, but here it is. So give thanks for the fact that you have a warm bed to recoup in, and people at work who will fill your shoes until you return. It's true that you didn't choose to have a flat tire, but thankfully your tires are now in tip-top shape for the trip you need to make next week. And on it goes. Thankfulness has a way of multiplying once you begin to put it to work.

AIN'T GOD GOOD!

By all external measures, Eloise and Coleman Lott have more reasons to be downcast than thankful. At seventy-nine, Eloise has had her share of misfortune. When she was just eleven her right leg became infected and required nearly three dozen surgeries throughout her life. A horrible electrical accident in her own yard claimed the life of her first husband.

As a teenager her daughter became paralyzed from the chest down, and her son died at the age of forty-five!

Coleman has also suffered many misfortunes. He lost his first wife when she was murdered in a robbery. Leukemia and bone marrow issues have weakened him physically, and near-blindness has made daily tasks very difficult. No doubt about it, these two folks have lots of troubles!

But how do the Lotts approach life? They continue to express appreciation for their "untold blessings." Eloise uses poetry to write about those blessings and her desire to have a positive attitude:

When my time comes,
*   this world to depart*
I would like it to be said:
*   "She lived with a happy heart."*

The Lotts sum up their philosophy of life with the words of Christian comedian Jerry Clower: "Ain't God good!"[7]

Clearly it's all a matter of perspective.

Make yours thankful!

◆ POINTS TO PONDER ◆

1. Remembering the church in Thessalonica, how can being thankful help you when facing difficult circumstances?

2. List some of the physical and emotional benefits of thankfulness. Can you identify benefits that you have experienced personally?

3. Describe the alternative to being thankful. Do you know people who consistently choose the cup-half-empty perspective on life? How does that affect the way they relate to other people and how others view them?

4. Have you ever consistently begun or ended your day by being thankful? How have you expressed your thanks? What has it done for you?

5. What does it mean to be thankful for little things? Name some of the little things that blessed you today.

6. How does consistently writing down the things you're thankful for contribute to an optimistic view of life?

7. Have you ever tried random acts of gratitude?

8. How could you apply a "praise the Lord anyway" attitude to specific challenges that you currently face?

TEST YOURSELF ON THANKFULNESS

Please READ the following statements and ask yourself, **"Do I agree that this describes me—my thoughts and actions during the last few months?"** Then, CIRCLE a number on the scale (below) from 1 to 10, showing how strongly you disagree or agree that each statement does or does not apply to you. Thus, a "1" means that you totally disagree that this is a strength in your life and a "perfect 10" means that you totally agree that the statement describes one of your strengths.

Totally Disagree	Very Strongly Disagree	Strongly Disagree	Somewhat Disagree	Slightly Disagree	Slightly Agree	Somewhat Agree	Strongly Agree	Very Strongly Agree	Totally Agree
1	2	3	4	5	6	7	8	9	10

1. I often thank God outwardly for His blessings.	1 2 3 4 5 6 7 8 9 10
2. I'm thankful every day that God protects and provides.	1 2 3 4 5 6 7 8 9 10
3. I am the most thankful person on the planet.	1 2 3 4 5 6 7 8 9 10
4. I am a completely grateful person.	1 2 3 4 5 6 7 8 9 10
5. I often show my gratitude for God's grace.	1 2 3 4 5 6 7 8 9 10
6. I often fail to be thankful for small blessings.	1 2 3 4 5 6 7 8 9 10
7. It's not possible to be thankful in my situation.	1 2 3 4 5 6 7 8 9 10
8. I really find it difficult to be thankful to other people.	1 2 3 4 5 6 7 8 9 10
9. I can't be grateful when there is so much pain in my life.	1 2 3 4 5 6 7 8 9 10
10. I do not show thankfulness to God most of the time.	1 2 3 4 5 6 7 8 9 10
TOTAL SCORE (Read directions) =	

SCORING CHART FOR THANKFULNESS

(Mark a line through the location of your score)

10 15 20 25 **30**...35 **38** 40 41 42 **43** 44 45 46 **47** 48 49 50 **51**...55...60

INTERPRETING YOUR SCORE: The middle point (43) represents the average score obtained by typical readers. Below-average scores are 38 or less, and those below 30 are extremely low. Above-average scores are 47 or more, and scores above 51 are extremely high.

If your score is below average, discuss your results with a friend and see if you can identify possible areas of improvement in thankfulness.

Chapter Five

*If we have not quiet in our minds, outward comfort will do
no more for us than a golden slipper on a gouty foot.*

JOHN BUNYAN

Content makes poor men rich; discontentment makes rich men poor.

BENJAMIN FRANKLIN

It was midnight in the prison, but no one was sleeping. It wasn't
unusual for new detainees to make a ruckus, but…what were those
sounds drifting up from The Hole—the inner, most secure part of
the prison?

Could it be singing?

All the prisoners were listening. It hadn't taken long for the gossip to
travel from cell to cell. Innocent of any wrongdoing, these guys had
been beaten without mercy and fastened in stocks. And for what?
Something about casting a demonic spirit out of a slave girl.

Unjustly and illegally beaten, shackled, and imprisoned, Paul and
Silas were doing the one thing that their hearts always defaulted to—
praying and singing hymns to God. Were they delusional? Why weren't
they plotting their defense—or at least demanding their rights as

Roman citizens? Surely they could have received some much-needed medical attention for their wounds and bruises.

Yet they were content to let God champion their cause.

Let's be honest. If this had been me, I would have been working up a sweat raking my cup across the bars of my cell. "When do I get my phone call? You're gonna hear from my lawyer!" No hymns for me. Anger, pouting, threats, schemes, and off-the-charts stress—but no hymns.

Can you imagine what it would be like to face those unexpected trials of life with the sort of calm optimism Paul and Silas had in this situation? Is that kind of contentment actually within reach?

Absolutely.

Absolutely, that is, if you understand the *what* and *how* of it.

SQUARE ONE

Contentment is one of those realities everybody longs for.

Ironic, isn't it? Striving for contentment? Simply understood, *contentment* means to be at ease with who you are, where you are, and what you have. It means that you are comfortable with your position and possessions, not needing more or different, bigger or better to make you happy. You are conTENT with your CONtent—that is, you have quietness of mind about your present condition.

What are we advocating here? Some kind of passive, whistle-in-the-dark fatalism? *Que Sera, Sera, whatever will be, will be....*

Not at all. True contentment does not mean settling for second best or approaching your world with grim and stoic resignation. Nor does it describe living life in a hammock in your backyard—although we could probably do a bit more of that and less of our frantic running around! Being at ease isn't an excuse for laziness. You still have to mow your lawn (sorry about that!).

What does contentment mean, then? It means you have an approach to life that allows you to be relaxed inside as you walk through whatever comes your way.

If the concept here is easy to grasp, why is the reality so elusive?

It's because, if we're not careful, what contentment we do possess can be stolen away from us. And there's a seasoned band of thieves out there waiting to do just that.

MUG SHOTS IN THE HALL OF DISCONTENT

The array of burglars that steal our contentment is long and ugly and all too familiar. Walk with me for a moment down the long Hall of Discontent and let's identify a few of the usual suspects.

Advertising

Here's one mug we recognize immediately. When you get right down to it, most of the programming on television exists because of ads. The shows we enjoy are mere hooks to get us to watch the main event—that is, the commercials. Every year corporate America pours *billions* of dollars into Hollywood-grade commercials that have one underlying purpose: to make you discontented and unhappy with where you are, who you are, and what you have.

Why would you want your old bucket of bolts when you could drive a newer, later model? Why would you settle for nondescript sneakers when you could own a pair like those worn by a basketball star?

Before you saw the ads, you were quite comfortable in your paid-for-albeit-not-so-new car. And your shoes? Hey, they were getting you around just fine, although…now that you think about it, perhaps they are a bit tired. And that twinge in your back this morning is undoubtedly the result of a mattress that should probably be replaced, perhaps with that high-tech one that so many "stars" seem to be using these days.

Before the ads hit your head, you were at ease with these issues of life. But now you see things differently. Now you're discontent. And what the advertisers hope will scratch that inner itch of yours is to rush out and buy their product or service.

Media

Here's another all-too-familiar mug.

In some ways, the media itself is an even more potent source of discontent than advertising. Consider the stories in your morning paper or on the nightly TV news. How many of them inspire you, give you hope, or make you feel thankful and blessed to live in the community? On the other hand, how many make you anxious, angry, or discouraged about something that may have been little more than pure speculation?

Sometimes early warnings of potential disasters are helpful, like when tracking a potential hurricane, alerting people to prepare. But how much of the "news" is more like Y2K, getting and keeping people on high alert for something that will never take place? For that matter, does ending our day by listening to news of more identity thefts, meth labs, and another case of child sex abuse really help us drift off to slumber land?

Comparison

Here's a most despicable thief!

No other felon has been more responsible for stealing contentment from human hearts. When we see programs on TV featuring the "rich and famous," we realize just how broke and ordinary we are! While they're jetting around the world sampling exotic pleasures, we're fighting traffic to get to Grandma's, feeling fortunate that the motel has promised to leave the light on for us. Perhaps if we lived our lives in isolation, we'd never have to deal with the challenge of comparison, but when we open our eyes, there it is! And it's bigger, newer, flashier, and ever-so-much-more exciting than ours!

My friend Ralph tells the story of something that happened to him one evening at a neighborhood party. At the time, he lived in a very nice area, definitely on the upper side of middle class. Most people would be quite happy to hang their shingle on any of the houses in his little subdivision, tucked into the woods, backing onto a beautiful stream.

On this particular occasion the neighborhood potluck was held at the newest, largest house in the immediate area. Everybody was excited to see the inside of the house they had only observed while under construction. When the party ended, as Ralph was walking with a neighbor under the starlight, the man shook his head and exclaimed dejectedly, "Guess I'll go home and throw rocks at my house!"

Until he entered the new house, the man had been quite satisfied. But in a matter of mere minutes his own house had become chopped liver. A disappointment. All because of that dreaded contentment thief *comparison*.

And so it goes, with one mug shot after another in that gray, dreary Hall of Discontent. Other unsettling factors like *unrealistic expectations, debt, and the insatiable need to have more-newer-better,* always keep you striving. It seems like the entire world is set up to rip the rug of contentment right out from under you. And perhaps it is. So what can be done to gain the kind of contentment experienced by Paul and Silas, who found themselves in a situation that should have been infuriating at best?

Let's take a little stroll outside. Enough of the drab, hopeless confines of the Hall of Discontent! Let's find a back door and step out of the dim light and stale air into the sunshine and fresh spring breezes of true contentment.

KEYS TO THE SECRET GARDEN

Do you remember the childhood classic *The Secret Garden*? Life changed for several children when they found the key to a long-neglected garden, once filled with color, joy, and beauty.

The Bible gives us keys—several of them—to the often-neglected Garden of Contentment in our lives. Each key is a principle, and each principle will open the door to a place of rest, peace, and freedom from envy, resentment, and self-pity. As we live our lives in the light of these principles, feelings of striving and discontent dissipate and fade away.

Principle #1: Delight comes from within.

Beware putting your hope in circumstances! Your life situations, whatever they may be, do not generate contentment. That's because contentment comes from *within*. Obviously Paul and Silas weren't in the best of situations in a dungeon with their feet locked in stocks. The tourist brochures of Philippi hadn't spoken of any place like that! Yet they were content; they were making the best of their situation, however agonizing and confining it must have been. They chose delight over despair. Imprisonment was an opportunity to reach a whole new group for Christ! They had a captive audience—literally—and they made the most of it. That's contentment.

Principle #2: Contentment is learned.

The Bible says you learn contentment through time and testing. It doesn't sneak up on you. It doesn't descend upon you out of the clear blue. Early in his ministry Paul faced formidable obstacles and afflictions. On his first missionary journey alone he was thrown out of three towns and beaten to the point of death in another.

His response? "I have learned to be content, whatever the circumstances may be. I know now how to live when things are difficult and I know how to live when things are prosperous. In general and in particular I have learned the secret of eating well or going hungry—of facing either plenty or poverty. I am ready for anything through the strength of the one who lives within me" (Philippians 4:11–13, Phillips). Either Paul was going to cultivate contentment or he was going to have to choose another profession!

Although contentment is learned, it is not necessarily learned easily! I once read about a family that became schooled in this quality when they were teetering on the edge of bankruptcy. As they surveyed their future, they concluded that if they were exceedingly frugal, they could repay the lion's share of the debts in five years. But that meant drastic changes in their lives, including wearing the same clothing year after year, choosing not to visit shopping malls, eliminating television shows that highlighted what they were missing, and developing simple pleasures like going for walks and picnicking in the park.

After several years of this rigid frugality, when they had paid off the last of their debts, they came to an amazing conclusion. They actually *preferred* their new lifestyle! They were far more content! The things they used to *need* they now didn't even *want*. But reaching that point began with a steep learning curve.[1]

This family learned through difficult circumstances something that would benefit us all. If we truly want contentment, then we need to evaluate the way we are living our lives, determining what things actually sabotage the contentment we desire. Then we make the decision to change the habits and commitments that get in the way.

Principle #3: God-sufficiency

When you put your faith in Jesus Christ, you are no longer alone. Ever. He has promised to never leave you nor forsake you, that He will be with you always even to the end of the age, when the stars fall from the sky. That means that when you go through trials, when you find yourself chin-deep in confusion, pain, and disappointment, He's right there with you. When you are up against seemingly insurmountable odds, He's there, doing what only He can do. Your sufficiency or contentment, then, is not in yourself, but in Him! *That's* why you can be comfortable, at ease, because you know that God will do whatever He desires to work things for your good and His glory.

No doubt that is why Paul, after having stated that he had learned to be content, then adds: "I can do all things through Christ who strengthens me" (Philippians 4:13). As Paul says elsewhere, "If God is for us, who can be against us?" (Romans 8:31).

Who, indeed.

It's comforting to realize that the God who spun a galaxy of galaxies into the majestic sea of space is the same God who is at this very moment at work on your behalf. He has committed Himself to seeing through to completion the work He began in your life.

Principle #4: Keep it in perspective.

Make no mistake, there will always be irritants in your life.

But they will pass away.

And they don't have to steal your joy.

A car stereo system you can hear a block away, a neighbor's leaf blower switched on at six on a Saturday morning when you were planning to sleep in, a nonstop barking dog, or an older gentleman driving in front of you at 45 in a 50 mph zone aren't really worth getting worked up about.

Put it in perspective. A friend of mine was fond of saying, "What difference is it going to make in a hundred years?" The answer? Probably not much. The real truth is that many of the things we find so irritating are in fact our own creation. If the irritated driver had left home without cutting his time short, he'd probably never have noticed the elderly man driving under the speed limit. But with only a thin sliver of time to make his meeting, all the traffic signals must turn green in his favor, everybody in front of him must go at least the speed limit, and at each merging point on the freeway, he needs to go first! In so many cases, we are the greatest enemies of our own contentment.

Principle #5: Worry is worse than worthless.

If you are going to have a contented approach to life, you simply cannot be a worrywart. This is so very basic that Jesus addressed it in His first public sermon. The words may be very familiar to you…but pretend you're reading them for the first time.

> *"Do not worry about your life, what you will eat or what you will drink; nor about your body, what you will put on. Is not life more than food and the body more than clothing? Look at the birds of the air, for they neither sow nor reap nor gather into barns; yet your heavenly Father feeds them. Are you not of more value than they? Which of you by worrying can add one cubit to his stature? So why do you worry about clothing? Consider the lilies of the field, how they grow: they neither toil nor spin; and yet I say to you that even Solomon in all his glory was not arrayed like one of these. Now if God so clothes the grass of the field, which today is, and tomorrow is thrown into the oven, will He not much more clothe you, O you of little faith? Therefore do not worry, saying, 'What shall we eat?' or 'What shall we drink?' or 'What shall we wear?' For after all these things the Gentiles seek. For your heavenly Father knows that you need all these things. But seek first the kingdom of God and His righteousness, and all these things shall be added to you." (Matthew 6:25–33)*

Not only does worry not add to your life, it *subtracts* from it. How can you experience contentment if you are uptight about the little things in your life? Is God in control or isn't He? Does He have a plan for your life, or doesn't He? Does He think good thoughts about you or doesn't He?

Principle #6: Eternal perspective

Finally, the people who are most contented are those who have an eternal perspective. They know they are about their Father's work, building up treasures that last forever. Everything they are and everything they do is in the light of eternity. Living with that understanding allows them to experience a level of rest and comfort others can only long for.

As with every other character quality, a little bit of contentment whets your appetite for more. Whether it is through simplifying your life or delighting in the little things or remembering that God is with you no matter what, as you learn contentment it calms your otherwise jangled nerves.

There's a wonderful story from the 1880s about a woman named Louisa Stead. As a young woman, she wanted to be a missionary to China but, due to health issues, had to stay in the United States. She ultimately married Mr. Stead, and as time passed they had a daughter they named Lily.

When Lily was just four years old, they took a little vacation at a nearby beach. One day while they were lounging on the sand, they suddenly realized that a young boy was drowning in the ocean. Without giving a second thought, Mr. Stead plunged into the water and swam out to the boy in the hope of rescuing him. The boy ended up pulling Mr. Stead underwater and both of them drowned, while Louisa and Lily watched helplessly.

Not being people of means, Louisa was left penniless, with no viable means of support. All she had to rely on was God, and that she did! One day when the cupboards were absolutely bare, with no food in the house or money to buy some, she opened her front door and found someone had left both groceries and money for her and her daughter. She was so overwhelmed by the graciousness of the Lord that she sat down and wrote a song that summed up the source of her contentment:

> 'Tis so sweet to trust in Jesus,
> Just to take Him at His Word;
> Just to rest upon His promise,
> Just to know, "Thus saith the Lord."
>
> Jesus, Jesus, how I trust Him!
> How I've proved Him o'er and o'er
> Jesus, Jesus, precious Jesus!
> O for grace to trust Him more!

Contentment, being at ease with where you are and what you have, enables you to face life's most difficult circumstances free from the anxiety that drains life from you and the worry that sabotages your happiness. Once you begin to experience it, you will never want to return to the discontentment treadmill.

Open the gate to that neglected garden in your life. Feel the breeze on your face and the sunshine on your shoulders. Relax your knotted muscles and rest your racing thoughts.

Louisa Stead was right.

The only thing we really need is grace to trust Him more.

◆ POINTS TO PONDER ◆

1. What does it mean to be content? Do you consider yourself consistently content?

2. What gets in the way of contentment for you? What "contentment thieves" are at work in your life? Do the same ones hit you repeatedly, or are they always changing?

3. How could you change your approach to life to protect yourself from these thieves? Detail specific steps you can take, like having a "fast" from news every third weekend.

4. Is it possible to separate your contentment from your circumstances? What do you need to do so that one isn't dependent on the other?

5. Are you learning to be content, or are you settling for discontentment in too many areas of your life? Are there specific situations you can use as contentment-learning opportunities?

6. What role does God's presence in your life play in your contentment?

7. Do you make mountains out of molehills—give certain irritants in your life far too much power to cause you distress?

8. Are you a worrywart? How does worry help you? How does it hurt?

9. Do you live each day in the light of eternity, keeping everything in perspective?

TEST YOURSELF ON CONTENTMENT

Please READ THE following statements and ask yourself, **"Do I agree that this describes me—my thoughts and actions during the last few months?"** Then, CIRCLE a number on the scale (below) from 1 to 10, showing how strongly you disagree or agree that each statement does or does not apply to you. Thus, a "1" means that you totally disagree that this is a strength in your life and a "perfect 10" means that you totally agree that the statement describes one of your strengths.

Totally Disagree	Very Strongly Disagree	Strongly Disagree	Somewhat Disagree	Slightly Disagree	Slightly Agree	Somewhat Agree	Strongly Agree	Very Strongly Agree	Totally Agree
1	2	3	4	5	6	7	8	9	10

1. I am content with all aspects of my life.	1 2 3 4 5 6 7 8 9 10
2. God gives me strength to be content in all circumstances.	1 2 3 4 5 6 7 8 9 10
3. I have a strong feeling of contentment in relationships.	1 2 3 4 5 6 7 8 9 10
4. I am a contented person because I believe God is faithful.	1 2 3 4 5 6 7 8 9 10
5. I'm content because I know God provides and protects.	1 2 3 4 5 6 7 8 9 10
6. I feel deep contentment while completing daily tasks.	1 2 3 4 5 6 7 8 9 10
TOTAL SCORE (Read directions) =	

SCORE YOURSELF ON CONTENTMENT

Take each of the numbered responses you circled, and add up the numbers to make a total score. For example, if you answered "6" to all

6 questions, the total would be 36. Write the total in the box below the questions, and also mark the location of your score on the chart below:

SCORING CHART FOR CONTENTMENT

(Mark a line through the location of your score)

6 10 15 20 **25** 30 **35**...40 41 42 **43** 44 45 46 **47** 48 49 **50** 55 57 60

INTERPRETING YOUR SCORE: The middle point (43) represents the average score obtained by typical readers. Below-average scores are 35 or less, and those below 25 are extremely low. Above-average scores are 47 or more, and scores above 50 are extremely high.

If your score is below average, discuss your results with a friend and see if you can identify possible areas of improvement in contentment.

Chapter Six

The key to everything is patience.
You get the chicken by hatching the egg, not by smashing it.

ARNOLD H. GLASOW

I am extraordinarily patient,
provided I get my own way in the end.

MARGARET THATCHER

Patience?

Let's face it, our feet of clay are firmly planted in the present, and we want results before this moment slips away.

How different it would be if we had God's perspective. Since He is timeless, He sees the whole picture all at once, and since He is Spirit, He perceives both the natural and spiritual realms in one view.

It may sound silly, but think of life as a parade with you standing on the curb watching the parade go by. You watch the drum major pass by and turn the corner up the street, out of sight. That portion of the "life parade" is now past. It happened and you experienced it. What is present in the "life parade" are the floats and bands that drift or march along right in front of you. Eventually the scoopers that clean up after the horses will sweep the street, but for now they are in the future.

You experience each of these views or events one at a time, but God is "in the blimp" above the parade route and sees the whole thing stretched out before Him. There is no beginning, middle, or end; He observes the entire panorama at once. His perspective is eternal.

God desires to give us a perspective that is more like His. He wants us to realize He has the whole parade, all of our lives, in control, and we can begin to experience the peace and patience He has for all of us. So how might that work?

MORE THAN JUST "ENDURING"

When most of us think of patience, we think about a willingness to put up with things that annoy or irritate us, bearing them without losing our temper. But real patience is a state of mind and heart where ration is elevated over passion, light over heat. Because we are patient, we remain calm and composed when things aren't necessarily going according to our plan, timetable, or desire.

That doesn't mean we *enjoy* whatever we're facing; it means we remain peaceful and unruffled in the face of delay, instead of getting angry and acting out rashly. We wait and keep our cool without becoming agitated.

Doesn't that sound wonderful?

Why is patience so simple and straightforward on paper, but so difficult to express when the traffic signal is malfunctioning and you're dangerously late to your appointment? Why is your fuse so short when you know your kids' mistakes are unintentional, like the keystroke that sent your presentation into cyberspace the night before the big meeting?

TEN REASONS FOR IMPATIENCE

There are more reasons for impatience than fleas on a dog. If you score low in patience, don't be impatient with yourself! Actually, you're in good company. The first step toward developing this quality is to identify the things that can get in the way.

#1: We're too self-centered.

Can you say, *It's all about me*? When we see ourselves as the epicenter of life, with everything revolving around us, it's understandably irritating when things don't progress the way we planned. We drum our fingers on the table in the waiting room of the doctor's office, thinking, *My schedule is just as important as yours. In fact, I have a schedule and clearly you don't!*

Whether we would actually articulate it, our behavior betrays the belief that all life revolves around us. We allow ourselves to respond with impatience, especially when we have to deal with others who think it's all about them.

#2: We're captives of the quick fix.

Delayed gratification? Are you kidding? As with a variety of things in our lives, we want patience and we want it *now*. In our microwave age, we have come to expect everything to happen in a New York minute. Why shouldn't we? Even crimes are solved in sixty minutes—and that includes the commercials!

Why should we go through the hassle of tilling up and preparing our soil to plant grass seed when we can bring in sod and have instant lawn? Why should we exercise and change our diet when there is a parade of diet pills that promise the desired effect? Isn't there a quick and easy way to get in shape and look great without giving up donuts?

For years I have waited for science to invent a "buff" pill so I don't have to work out several times a week, and frankly, I'm losing patience!

It used to be that we telephoned a friend, and if they were talking to somebody else, we'd get a busy signal and call back later. Now we beep in and electronically demand to be heard, like a toddler pulling on his mommy's skirt. Failing that, we try their cell phone. What difference if they are in the middle of a colon screening?

Is it any wonder we get impatient with a difficult marriage and reject the idea of several months of counseling? Can't we just fix it in one or two quick appointments?

#3: We don't see the big picture.

When my dad was getting up in years, he fell and broke his hip. During his recovery he was placed in a fabulous rehabilitation unit in his city. The well-trained staff knew exactly how to work with his issues and facilitated his recovery in a remarkable way. As I watched what they did, it struck me that my own community needed a rehab center like this one. How could that come about?

I began to work on the project, doing whatever I could to instigate the development of such a center. Several people in the community had similar concerns, and in reasonably short order, we formed a committee to draft a proposal to present to the hospital board. I chaired the committee.

I looked forward to the first meeting, envisioning the project as complete before it had even been clarified on paper. But what a let-down! The meeting was nothing like I had anticipated, and I left bemoaning that if this project ever got off the ground, it wouldn't be finished in my lifetime!

Later, a fellow committee member taught me a lesson that would serve me well. She had worked quite successfully with committees and governmental agencies for years, and suggested that if we patiently crafted a plan that would be best for the community, lots of other people would support the concept, and we would get the results we'd hoped for.

What a concept! I took her advice, learned my lesson, and even though it took considerably longer than I would have wanted, we ended up with a rehab center that has been a remarkable addition to our community. I learned a lesson: Keep your eye on the big picture.

#4: We have unresolved personal issues.

Have you ever been tied up in knots about something at work, and dragged those feelings home with you to take out on your spouse, your children, or the family dog? Your son asks the simple question, "Dad, did you remember to pick up my uniform at the cleaners?" and you bark out, "Why must I always be the errand boy?"

It's common to project the emotions from one area of our lives onto other unrelated areas or situations. When we don't deal with the true source of our frustrations, we can become short-tempered and behave in ways that are definitely uncalled for.

#5: We are pushed by the pace of our culture.

No matter where we turn today, everything seems rushed. It's silly and old-fashioned to put film in the camera and wait to get pictures developed when we can snap them digitally and print them instantly at home. There's less and less need to meet people face-to-face, when we have fax machines and videoconferencing. With everything happening so quickly, as if on cue, is it any wonder we become impatient when we have to wait for something? If there's an unexpected delay, somebody in the chain must not be multitasking!

#6: We are victims of our own poor planning.

Although we get impatient having to fight all the traffic on the bridge to get to the doctor's appointment, the truth is we could have made the appointment for a time when we know the bridge has less traffic. Instead of arriving at the restaurant before the dinner crowd, we get angry when there's a forty-five minute wait. The reason for the impatience? Our own poor planning!

#7: We carry unrealistic expectations.

Think about the young parents who decide to take their three-year-old with them to a movie. Everything's fine until the three-year-old starts behaving like a three-year-old. She is restless, curious, and talkative. You hear her voice above the sound track and watch as her parents hurry her up the aisle for the fourth time to take her potty. What started out as cute becomes a source of irritation for the parents and the others in the theater.

But who created this problem?

Not the little girl! It was simply the wrong venue for an outing with a young child. If mom and dad had taken little Precious to the park, it would have been lots of fun. For everybody!

#8: We get overcommitted.

Why is it when somebody asks us to do something, especially someone we know and love, it's impossible to say no? A nod here and there isn't so bad. It's when we string a series of yeses together that we get into trouble. Essentially, we plan our own train wreck. When it comes time to follow through, there simply isn't enough time in a day to make everybody happy. As a result, we get impatient, frustrated, and even angry.

Yet—once again—where does the problem lie? With the people in our lives? Not at all. They're really innocent bystanders! The problem lies with ourselves and our unwillingness to discipline our commitments. We are the source of our own irritation.

#9: We fail to account for the complexity of life.

There may have been a time when life was simple. But that time is barely visible in the rearview mirror. Even though time-saving technology abounds, life gets more complicated by the day. We have privacy acts that protect us so efficiently that they create roadblocks for people who want to lend a helping hand. It used to be that if your elderly parent was facing a health problem, you could talk with his physician, get an understanding of his condition, and embark on a course of action. Now we have privacy laws that make it impossible to "get there from here." Our complex lives test our patience!

#10: We have too many things demanding our attention.

Think about all the things ringing, pulsing, buzzing, blinking, humming, chirping, vibrating, and crying out for your *immediate* attention. What are you to do? You have to answer! It may be the police saying your daughter has been in a wreck. (Forget the fact that she's happily married and living in another state with her husband and two kids!) While the chances of that being true are less than your being hit by lightning, nonetheless the thought is there.

Better answer that phone. Now. But if you do, your dinner will get cold, you'll lose your train of thought on the proposal you're writing, the mailman will go by before you can get that "rush" package to him, or you'll forget where you were reconciling the bank statement. Is it any wonder you might get a bit frustrated and lose your patience?

TEN TIPS TO CULTIVATE PATIENCE

So what are we to do? How can we ever hope to develop patience? Believe it or not, it can happen.

#1: Live your life with both feet on solid ground.

Approach each day with the knowledge that God has a plan for your life. He is in control even when you aren't. Be confident that "He who has begun a good work in you will complete it until the day of Jesus Christ" (Philippians 1:6).

Remember that God is God, and you aren't.

He controls the universe, and you don't.

He's done quite a good job thus far, and there's no reason to believe that's going to change. He will enable you to deal with any challenge you face, no matter how big or small. But you must cling tenaciously to this fact and carry it with you into each situation. It's amazing what a calming effect it will have on your heart.

#2: Make a realistic appraisal of your situation.

How did you end up where you are? Is there a good reason for your frustration? Is getting upset really going to help solve your problem? Wouldn't it be better to think through some more productive ways to deal with your situation?

Aron Ralston tells an incredible story of calm assessment and productive planning. Aron is a young man who saved his own life by cutting off part of his arm. He had been hiking alone in a wilderness area and slid down an incline, dislodging some rocks. Ultimately his arm was pinned by a boulder weighing hundreds of pounds. He was miles away from civilization, in a ravine where he might not be found for months. What was he to do?

Without patience and the will to rise above the pain and uncertainty, he never would have been able to accomplish what he did. Somehow Aron was able to engage his mind and slowly but surely design a plan. He figured out how to apply a tourniquet to cut off the blood flow to his pinned arm, then slowly sawed off his arm with a pocket knife! Once free, he hiked several miles before encountering people who helped him get to civilization and medical care.[1]

A realistic appraisal of his situation enabled him to patiently, methodically achieve his objective.

#3: Consider the benefits of waiting.

When Betty and I located our first house, we were really excited. We toured several houses and answered a number of newspaper ads, looking for a place just right for us. Finally we found a house that would work. It was fairly new, in great shape, and didn't even need any painting. We discussed its virtues all the way home and called our realtor immediately upon arrival.

She then went to work on our behalf and quickly brought us all the details, including an offer sheet ready for us to sign. Unfortunately, the price of the house was more than we wanted to spend. While we were new to the whole real estate thing, we had established what we would be willing to carry for a mortgage, and had communicated that clearly before we had begun our search.

The realtor brushed that off, assuring us it wasn't all that much more than we were comfortable with, and in a year or two, assuming salary increases, we would never notice the higher payment. I must admit, it was tempting.

Still, we stuck with our original decision and told the realtor it wouldn't work. "If somebody else wants that house," we told her, "maybe God has a better one for us."

We didn't get that house. But in a matter of weeks a friend told us about a neighbor selling his house, and he was willing to show it to us before it even went on the market. When we got there, we fell in love with the place. It had far more to commend it than the other house, and it was within our price range!

Clearly there were great benefits to waiting patiently.

#4: Appreciate the value of controlling your temper.

The easiest thing in the world is to give place to your emotions. But you might not like where that takes you! Recently here in Washington, a woman reacted to a bad hair day by giving free rein to her emotions. She was so upset over a bad haircut that she returned to the salon and demanded to see her hairstylist. Since the stylist wasn't in yet, the unhappy client returned to her car to wait.

When the stylist arrived, the client pulled a gun on her, walked her into the salon, and demanded her $100 back. She then returned to the parking lot, shot out the back window of the stylist's car, and threw her gun through the window she'd just blown to bits. Leaving the lot, she immediately drove to another hair salon where she proceeded to get a trim, calmly chatting with the new stylist about her grandkids and her bad haircut. She paid with the money she had just stolen.

Needless to say, the impatient woman was arrested and taken to jail when she emerged from salon number two. The decision to give free expression to her frustrated feelings proved to be disastrous. If only she'd decided to rise above her emotions! As Solomon says, "He who sows iniquity will reap sorrow, and the rod of his anger will fail" (Proverbs 22:8).

#5: Get a handle on the things that irritate you.

Make a mental list of the things that annoy you and consider how you might handle them when you encounter them again. As you review your list, remember that irritants aren't necessarily all bad. Remember how pearls are created? A mollusk is irritated by a little parasite, so it produces a substance to coat the intruder and make the irritant smooth. Layer upon layer of the smoothing material settles over the surface of the parasite, until the irritant is completely undetectable. And what do we find in its place? A pearl! What might happen if you take notice of your irritants and determine to smooth them over?

#6: Remember that sometimes you are the cause of another's frustration.

It's easy to get so consumed by the things that bother us that we lose sight of the fact that we ourselves can be annoying. (Imagine!) Have you ever been talking on your cell phone while driving, oblivious to the fact that traffic is backing up behind you? Have you ever taken many more than ten items into the ten-items-or-less lane at the grocery store? Sometimes we are the perpetrators and not always the victims of things that cause frustration. When we see the shoe on the other foot, it helps us not to be so impatient ourselves.

#7: Practice the ancient art of counting to ten.

Never mind that this is a prehistoric cliché. When you are ready to pull the trigger on your emotions, take a deep breath, step back, and count to ten. Slowly. As silly as it might seem, it allows you to separate your impulse from your action. It gives you time to think through your reaction and allow the Spirit rather than the flesh to be in control.

After the person has given you a piece of his mind, instead of lashing back, what might happen if you responded, "Wow, you have some strong feelings about this. What do you think I should do?" If your teenager has put a dent in the new car, or your coworker has taken personal credit for your "job well done," take a moment and let your mind take control and your heart rate slow down before you respond. You will be pleased with the result.

#8: Keep in mind that trials produce treasures.

This is true in every respect—physically, emotionally, and spiritually. Physically, you can't build muscle unless you work it, but you can't work it effectively without experiencing some pain. Emotionally, it's hard to be compassionate with somebody who is going through a tough situation unless you've experienced troubles yourself. Having faced trials, you have something significant to give to someone who's on the front end of the journey.

Focusing on the treasure that is ahead of you instead of the trial that is upon you, you will find patience that sustains you.

#9: Learn from God's object lessons.

James makes a great point: "Therefore be patient, brethren, until the coming of the Lord. See how the farmer waits for the precious fruit of the earth, waiting patiently for it until it receives the early and latter rain. You also be patient" (5:7–8).

While he is talking about having patience to wait for the Lord's return in a disintegrating and destructive world, the principle clearly applies to all of life. There is no way a farmer could keep his sanity apart from patience. Once the seed is in the ground, *how do you hurry it up?* It's all about waiting patiently.

#10: Recognize that patience has great rewards.

"Why don't you just throw the dumb thing away? If it hasn't bloomed in twenty-five years, it's not going to start now!"

It seemed self-evident to me. My mom had given Betty a start from her *Hoya*, a houseplant that produced fragrant flowers year round, and Betty had done everything imaginable to help her fledgling follow suit. Year after year she believed, "This is the treatment that will kick-start the continual blooming," and like Charlie Brown and the football, all she got was let down.

I have to admit, I hung in there pretty tenaciously for the first decade, believing the best about that little plant, but I had ultimately decided the effort was futile.

Once Betty saw a blossom peeking out of the leaves, only to discover that a friend had imported it from her own plant and strategically placed it on B's as a little joke. The *Hoya* had become such a project that one couple began secretly praying for it!

Then it happened. All of a sudden, after twenty-five years, that plant began to bloom! Did you catch that? Twenty-five years! Just a few blooms in the first season, as though it was making sure we were paying attention. Then it was off and running. Indeed, at the moment it sits happily in our dining room window blooming its little heart out with thirty or forty blooms. In the evening it releases its sweet fragrance as its way of saying, "Thanks for being patient with me. Here's a little gift."

Twenty-five years of waiting, watering, and wondering were clearly worth it all! Remarkable what patience can do for you.

Patience has so many benefits that it demands listing several. Among the rewards of patience are these:

- It diminishes our stress.
- It increases our ability to reason calmly.
- It enhances our peace of mind.
- It defuses anger.
- It improves our self-esteem.
- It lowers our blood pressure.
- It enables us to reach productive solutions.
- It makes us nicer people to be with, improving our relationship with others.
- It allows us to be more sensitive to the needs of others.
- It saves us from rash decisions and actions.
- It lightens our load of worry and responsibility.
- It reflects the Spirit of the Lord.

God develops patience in the life of the believer as a natural expression of His character in ours—it comes along with living a godly life as a "fruit of the Spirit."

"Rest in the LORD," David tells us, "and wait patiently for Him"

(Psalm 37:7). In other words, as He cultivates patience in us, we get to wait patiently in Him.

There is rest in that, the Bible tells us.

And impatience doesn't have a chance.

◆ POINTS TO PONDER ◆

1. Call to mind the last time you were impatient. Think about the circumstances surrounding it. What specifically led to your impatience? What control did you exert over the way you acted? How did your impatience affect the situation?

2. List some of the ways you see impatience being expressed today. Is it helping or hurting our society?

3. Review the ten reasons for impatience. Which are the most familiar to you? Are there others you'd like to add to the list? What can you learn from them?

4. Reconsider the ten tips to cultivate patience. Which specific ones do you need to work on? Are there others you could add to this list?

5. Jot down some specific benefits you have experienced by being patient. How would strengthening this quality enrich your life?

TEST YOURSELF ON PATIENCE

Please READ the following statements and ask yourself, **"Do I agree that this describes me—my thoughts and actions during the last few months?"** Then, CIRCLE a number on the scale (below) from 1 to 10, showing how strongly you disagree or agree that each statement does or does not apply to you. Thus, a "1" means that you totally disagree that this is a strength in your life and a "perfect 10" means that you totally agree that the statement describes one of your strengths.

Totally Disagree	Very Strongly Disagree	Strongly Disagree	Somewhat Disagree	Slightly Disagree	Slightly Agree	Somewhat Agree	Strongly Agree	Very Strongly Agree	Totally Agree
1	2	3	4	5	6	7	8	9	10

1. I patiently wait on God to help me in stressful times.	1 2 3 4 5 6 7 8 9 10
2. God gives me strength to be patient when I'm delayed.	1 2 3 4 5 6 7 8 9 10
3. I can peacefully endure long delays that are stressful.	1 2 3 4 5 6 7 8 9 10
4. I am a very patient person.	1 2 3 4 5 6 7 8 9 10
5. Other people say that I have been patient and "long-suffering" in life.	1 2 3 4 5 6 7 8 9 10
6. I can be patient even when people attack me.	1 2 3 4 5 6 7 8 9 10

The following statements express concerns about patience. Circle a LOW number if you disagree that this is a concern for you, or a HIGH number if you agree that this is a concern.

7. I do NOT do well with problems that take years to solve.	1 2 3 4 5 6 7 8 9 10
8. My motto is, "Don't delay— Do something fast!"	1 2 3 4 5 6 7 8 9 10
9. I can easily get impatient with stressful tasks.	1 2 3 4 5 6 7 8 9 10
10. I really suffer when important things are delayed.	1 2 3 4 5 6 7 8 9 10
TOTAL SCORE (Read directions) =	

SCORE YOURSELF ON PATIENCE

Take each of the numbered responses you circled, and add up the numbers to make a total score. For example, if you answered "6" to all 10 questions, the total would be 60. Write the total in the box below the questions, and also mark the location of your score on the chart below:

SCORING CHART FOR PATIENCE

(Mark a line through the location of your score)

10 25 30 35 **40** 45 50 **55** 60 61 62 63 64 **65** 66 67 68 69 70 **75** 80 **85** 90 95 100

INTERPRETING YOUR SCORE: The middle point (65) represents the average score obtained by typical readers. Below-average scores are 55 or less, and those below 40 are extremely low. Above-average scores are 75 or more, and scores above 85 are extremely high.

If your score is below average, discuss your results with a friend and see if you can identify possible areas of improvement in patience.

Chapter Seven

First keep the peace within yourself,
then you can also bring peace to others.

THOMAS À KEMPIS

V isualize world peace.

Okay, what's that all about? A command? Something like, "Do as I say and nobody gets hurt"?

I'd pulled up to a stoplight, and there it was. A demand on my mind that nearly brought on brain-lock, shattering the reverie of the warm Northwest evening and the smooth jazz sliding out my car radio. A bumper sticker like that ought to be illegal.

Visualize world peace? How, pray tell, do I do that? What color, shape, or texture would it be? Tall or short? Wide or narrow? Hot or cold? Up or down? Should that visualization include images of children holding hands, dancing in a meadow of wildflowers? Or maybe a clip of some multiethnic gathering with everyone exchanging sweet smiles?

Let's give the creator of the bumper sticker the benefit of the doubt. He was probably serious about promoting global peace. But what in the world did he have in mind? Was he suggesting everybody just think good thoughts and transmit good vibrations, so the world would magically settle into peace? Shades of John Lennon.

All we are saying is give peace a chance…

The tongue-in-cheek version of that bumper sticker appeared soon after the serious one hit the morning commute. When I first saw *Visualize Whirled Peas* I nearly drove off the road laughing! Now *that* I could do! I have kids, and I could remember what pureed veggies looked like. Visualizing world peace was impossible, but whirled peas? Hey, no problem at all.

Regardless of how it's promoted, everybody wants peace in the world. But achieving it? Well, that's quite another matter. I'm reminded of the false prophets in Jeremiah's day who kept "saying, 'Peace, peace!' when there is no peace" (Jeremiah 6:14).

And so it is today. As soon as a conflict simmers down in one area of the world, another heats up somewhere else. It's like trying to hold a dozen huge beach balls under the water all at once. You stretch yourself out horizontally in the water and manage to get three submerged—as nine more pop to the surface. In my own lifetime there hasn't been a moment truly free of tension in the world.

During the debacle in Vietnam, the peace protesters suggested the military lay down its weapons, send the soldiers home, and the world would be at peace.

Voila! Just like that.

Yet when the U.S. presence disappeared from Vietnam—when the last American chopper lifted off from that rooftop in Saigon, did peace descend on that city, that nation? Of course not.

The last thirty years have seen Russia invade Afghanistan, the Ayatollah grab hostages in Iran, and the Sandinistas try to eradicate the Contras. Iraq's invasion of Kuwait, as well as the ongoing conflicts and genocide in the Middle East, Bosnia, Rwanda, and the Sudan have all made world peace an unrealized dream.

In the aftermath of 9/11, a woman on a call-in talk show suggested the United States spend its entire military budget on humanitarian aid. You know, just let all the soldiers go home from everywhere and park all the tanks and fighters. That, she declared, would abolish terrorism. How naïve could she be? How would the presence of U.S. money nullify the conflicts festering in other nations? If people were, in fact, peace minded, they'd live that way!

But they are not. So they don't.

Even so…something in every (sane) person wants peace. We want peace in the world, in our nation, in our cities, on our streets, in our schools, neighborhoods, and homes. But wanting it and experiencing it…ah, those are two very different things. As with so many other longings of the human soul, peace is elusive. Just when we're on the cusp of experiencing it, something upsets the proverbial apple cart.

So…can we ever hope to know peace as a reality?

Yes.

Because peace is not an ideal, an illusion, or a concept. *Peace is a Person.*

PEACE IS A PERSON (NOT A PROGRAM)

The heart of the problem is the human heart. People generate conflicts that cannot be eradicated by treaties, contracts, resolutions, styles of government, and elected officials, because the heart problem always sabotages their best efforts. In the Bible Jeremiah said it this way: "The heart is deceitful above all things, and desperately wicked; who can know it?" (Jeremiah 17:9).

While none of us likes to admit our sinfulness or our deceitful hearts, we'll never run fast enough to run away from it. Wherever we go, it comes with us. It's in our DNA. Since Adam first tasted apple pie in the Garden, man has had a penchant for evil. Birds fly, fish swim, it rains in Seattle, and man does evil. Can you doubt that, after reading the front page of your newspaper? Outwardly we talk about peace, sing about peace, and even organize for peace, but inwardly we aren't built to make it happen.

That's the bad news.

But thank God, it isn't all bad news.

God Himself, the Creator of all, has given us the means to deal with our heart problem through a person, Jesus Christ. As we put our trust in Him, we get to start fresh, with brand-new hearts. Years before Jesus came to the earth, God foretold through the prophet Ezekiel: "I will give you a new heart and put a new spirit within you; I will take the heart of stone out of your flesh and give you a heart of flesh. I will put My Spirit within you and cause you to walk in My statutes, and you will keep My judgments and do them" (Ezekiel 36:26–27). That is precisely what came to pass in Jesus!

Try as we might by staging protests or forcing people (at gunpoint!) to lay down their weapons, there is no peace without a supernatural work of God through Jesus Christ. The absence of external hostilities does not produce internal peace. The peace that mankind longs for is a matter of the heart. Even the pagan philosopher Epictetus spoke wisely in the first century when he noted: "While the emperor may give peace from war on land and sea, he is unable to give peace from passion, grief and envy. He cannot give peace of heart, for which man yearns more than even for outward peace."

That yearning can only be satisfied through a relationship with the person Jesus Christ. He alone can do the transformation that brings about lasting peace. Peace is a person, not a program.

PEACE IS A PROMISE (NOT A PIPE DREAM)

While the world protests and plans for peace, those who love the Lord know peace and *live* in it...because of a promise. For them it's reality because of a relationship with the Promise Keeper. In the last hours before His crucifixion, Jesus spoke about this. During the Last Supper with His disciples, He said, "Peace I leave with you, My peace I give to you; not as the world gives do I give to you. Let not your heart be troubled, neither let it be afraid" (John 14:27). Moments later, He added: "These things I have spoken to you, that in Me you may have peace. In the world you will have tribulation; but be of good cheer, I have overcome the world" (John 16:33).

In both cases, He promised peace to His people. *My peace I give to you.* Could it be? Peace…a gift from Jesus Christ Himself? *In Me you may have peace.* Sign me up—I want that! Wait…. I know Jesus. I can *have* that—even in difficult situations!

Jesus had a "signature" statement that He used over and over: *Don't be afraid!* When His disciples were freaking out on a wild and stormy night at sea, thinking they would soon be fish bait, He calmed their hearts with *"Don't be afraid,"* then turned and calmly told the sea to take it easy.

Remember the story? The sea immediately reflected the same peace Jesus radiated. Notice He didn't start screaming at the sea or beating it with an oar: "You pipe down or I'm going to drain you dry!"

No, He calmly asked it to relax. The Bible uses a word for "calm" that is related to the word for "smile."

Responding to Jesus, the sea sighed and smiled. And that was that.

In another instance, a woman trembled with fear when Jesus discovered she had touched His robe. She'd been confident that she would be healed of the affliction that had drained her strength and finances for the previous twelve years—if she could only edge through the crowd and touch the hem of his garment!

Jesus turned to her and said, *"Don't be afraid!"* In other words, "It's okay, daughter. Everything's going to be fine." What a fabulous word of encouragement! And it was instantly true. She received His peace and complete healing besides.

A few pages later in the gospels, a father was beside himself because Jesus' disciples couldn't heal his little boy of seizures. Dad was desperate because sometimes the little guy had even fallen into a fire or water. Sooner or later he could have a fatal accident! When Jesus appeared on the scene, the poor guy frantically reached out for help. In response, Jesus very calmly said, *"Bring him here to Me."* And with that, He healed him. "Don't be afraid, dad, it's okay. I'm here. It's going to be fine!"

When Jesus promised peace, He produced it.

He didn't say, "Visualize peace," to that distraught father. He simply delivered it. And He hasn't changed His mode of operation to this day. His promise of peace still extends to all who trust in Him. It isn't merely a pipe dream; it's reality. It isn't a slogan or a bumper sticker on a Volvo or a political promise or an antiwar rock ballad or an unreachable star.

It's there. It's real. It works.

Why? Because *He* is there, *He* is real, and *He* works. And *He* produces what *He* promises!

This promise applies even when our world is shaken. Precisely in the midst of mayhem, Jesus gives us His peace.

In Psalm 46:1–2, it's as though the psalmist was being interviewed by a reporter, and the reporter asks him, "What's the most devastating set of circumstances you can imagine? What would be the very most frightening turn of events you could think of?"

The songwriter closes his eyes and leans back in his chair for a moment. "Well," he says, "how about if the ground under your feet suddenly gave way—like a giant sinkhole? That ought to do it. Or how about this? What if all the mountains in Israel were suddenly ripped from their places and dumped into the Great Sea—creating earthquakes, tidal waves, and all the rest?"

Okay," the reporter comes back, "what then? How would you react? Would you be out of your mind with fear? Would your bones turn to jelly?"

"No, not at all," the psalmist replies.

"What? How can you say that? The earth opening up beneath you? Mountains dumping into the sea? How could you not be afraid?"

"Because of God. He's my refuge. He's my strength. He's right there beside me in my times of trouble. The God of Jacob is my fortress."

Remember the two-sided promise that Jesus made to His followers: This side of heaven there will be difficulties (*tribulation*), but victory is Mine (*I have overcome the world*). That victory is an accomplished fact; we just have to walk through those difficulties to get there! God's peace is greater than any hardship we face.

My son Geoff was recently treated by a remarkable and compassionate surgeon who is fond of saying to anxious parents, "Everything's going to be fine!"

There's no hot air in that statement. No empty promises. This doctor *delivers*. Dr. Milton Waner surveys the condition of his patients, whose cases are frequently considered hopeless and impossible by other physicians. He then lifts up optimism and hope, even in the face of overwhelming odds. God has used his extraordinary skill to effect "impossible" healings, and has used this man's compassion to soothe many anxious hearts.

Little Aslynn Brown was born perfectly normal, save for a pale-red patch on one side of her pretty little head. Her parents were advised to put lotion on it to make it disappear. They followed instructions faithfully, but within a few weeks the pink patch had turned deep cranberry, becoming blistered and swollen. A few more weeks passed and the cranberry-colored lesion had spread to her neck, forming a thick, softball-sized mass that began to fold down her little ear.

As this sleeping giant continued to awaken, the skin of her ear and scalp began cracking and bleeding without warning. In no time at all, the creeping mass engulfed the back of her head, drooping over her upper back.

By the time they consulted with another doctor, the Browns were told they were too late. The hemangioma was too large to treat with steroids, too deep for lasers, and too risky for surgery. Nothing could be done. They were definitely at the end of their proverbial rope and could barely hang on.

Things went from bad to worse. Their little one had developed an enlarged heart from supplying the volume of blood necessary to feed the tumor, and the demand on her body had arrested her growth. The doctors could only put her on heart medication until the hemangioma disappeared, which perhaps would happen within eight to ten years, *if* she lived that long.

They say necessity is the mother of invention, but in this case it was the grandma who frantically searched the web and found Dr. Waner, then of Little Rock, Arkansas. The family took Aslynn to him for a consultation, and after his usual cooing and making over this struggling child, Dr. Waner said, "Oh, this is a big one. I can fix it!" Can you imagine the relief and hope those four little words produced? *"I can fix it."*

And he did.

A brief time later, at Beth Israel hospital in Manhattan, Dr. Waner removed the gnarled growth in one surgery. One surgery! Within five weeks, the murmur was barely detectable, and Aslynn was weaned off her heart medication. Not long after, Dr. Waner summed up the results saying, "Aslynn Brown is a perfect child!"[1]

"Everything's going to be fine."

Who doesn't want to hear those words, when the going gets tough? "Don't be afraid." Who doesn't want to exchange fear for assurance? "My peace I leave with you." Who doesn't want to receive a promise like that? It's great to know that a personal relationship with Jesus brings with it the promise of peace.

PEACE IS A PRODUCT, NOT A P

By its very nature, peace always rests on faith. We ne
where we check "peace" off our list and move on to
peace can either be assaulted by present circumstances or robbed by
future possibilities, but God gives us the ability to deal with both those
eventualities.

When situations blindside us, we can renew our peace by reviewing
the character and power of God, Who holds our lives in His capable
hands. "The heavens are Yours, the earth also is Yours; the world and all
its fullness, You have founded them.... You have a mighty arm; strong is
Your hand, and high is Your right hand. Righteousness and justice are
the foundation of Your throne; mercy and truth go before Your face"
(Psalm 89:11,13–14).

God's Word also holds the solution for anxieties about the future
that plague us: "Be anxious for nothing, but in everything by prayer and
supplication, with thanksgiving, let your requests be made known to
God; and the peace of God, which surpasses all understanding, will
guard your hearts and minds through Christ Jesus. Finally brethren,
whatever things are true, whatever things are noble, whatever things are
just, whatever things are pure, whatever things are lovely, whatever
things are of good report, if there is any virtue and if there is anything
praiseworthy—meditate on these things" (Philippians 4:6–8).

Like clouds in the Northwest, challenges and concerns are a part of
life. You hock your house to pay for Junior's orthodontia, and he
announces he's going out for football! That's why we never want to lose
sight of the fact that peace is a process, not a product. In those difficult
moments, present and future, we want to lean into the Spirit of the living God, remembering His promise to us: *Peace I leave with you, My
peace I give to you…let not your hearts be troubled!*

THE ENVELOPE, PLEASE

God has built powerful rewards into peace that whet our appetites and motivate us to develop a greater sense of His deep-down tranquility and rest in our lives.

What rewards? Try this one on. *Peace enhances our relationships.* When we have inner peace, it's a whole lot easier to be peaceful in our every contact through the day. We are motivated to believe the best about others, to solve problems peacefully, and to resolve conflicts promptly. We step back and look for the bigger picture, and choose our battles carefully.

The Bible teaches a direct correlation between peaceful relationships with people and with God. Even the effectiveness of our prayers can be hindered if the relationship with our spouse is out of order (see 1 Peter 3:7). The more we experience God's peace within, the more it will be expressed in our relationships.

Here's another reward. *Peace increases our productivity.* Think about the last time you got tied up in knots because of something that happened at work. You fretted and stewed about it, brought it up in conversations, even ended your evening with heartburn! How different things would have looked if you had exchanged your agitation for God's peace.

When Paul landed in Athens, still smarting from being booted out of Philippi, Thessalonica, and Berea, he had good reason to be discouraged. He hardly had time to plant churches in those cities before he became persona non grata, and was summarily deposited—with bruises, contusions, and lacerations—outside the city limits.

This apostle thing could be brutal.

What was worst, he'd been driven out of town before he got to build basic Christian principles into the lives of the new believers. What would happen to those precious babes in Christ? How long could they last in such a tender state—especially with all of those false teachers prowling around like so many slavering wolves.

As he languished in Athens by himself, he could have become quite despondent. But because he rested in the Lord, believing that God would be faithful to continue the work He had begun, Paul was able to pursue his ministry.

He was led of the Spirit to witness to some of the most formidable minds in the area—people who had never so much as heard the name of Jesus Christ. Had Paul been wrapped in emotional turmoil, distracted by the injustice of his own plight or worried sick about those new believers, he would not have sensed the leading of the Spirit. He would not have recognized the opportunity to preach about the "unknown God," the Lord of heaven and earth. But because he rested in God's peace, he ended up breaking entirely new ground for the gospel!

When you live your life in God's peace, you will have a whole lot more time and energy to be productive!

Here's another thought. *Peace makes us more attractive.* Who enjoys being around somebody who is always in crisis mode? Many years ago, Betty and I had a neighbor who came to be known in the neighborhood as "Frantic Fran." Her entire life was a frenzy. The kids better not be playing in the street when Hurricane Fran roared around the corner on two wheels, jamming the pedal to the metal for the home stretch. She would leap out of her car, sometimes not even bothering to shut the door, and bolt into the house. Before you knew it, she was flying back out to her car, slamming it into reverse, and laying rubber as she shoved it into drive and bucked her way down the street. It raised our blood pressure just to watch her!

I've got to be honest: That personality type is anything but winsome. I get nervous just thinking about her. Contrast that with the person who exudes the peace of the Lord. Now that is the kind of person I want to be with. And so does everybody else. Peace is attractive, and as you express it in your life, folks enjoy being in your presence. Isn't that how people felt about Jesus?

Finally, *peace catches on.* The only way the world will ever be at peace is when people experience God's peace through the Prince of Peace. That kind of peace will change the world, one heart at a time. Don't let another moment go by without thanking the Lord for the peace He has for you.

You don't have to visualize it. Just step into it and let it carry you.

And for goodness' sake, don't forget to pass it on! This world of ours needs all the peace it can get.

◆ POINTS TO PONDER ◆

1. Define peace. Do you think that "world peace" is possible to achieve?

2. Describe personal or inner peace as you experience it. Describe a situation in which you experienced a peace that truly did not come from your own ability to muster it.

3. Jesus commanded the sea, and it "smiled." When you're headed for "war" with your spouse or your teenager, what steps can you take to defang the situation—to calm the storm?

4. Think about a time when you were the one who caused a conflict to escalate. How was reason lost? What biblical principle or what specific Bible verse could you have brought to bear on the situation?

5. Peace is a Person and a promise, but it is something that the individual must seek and receive. Read 2 Timothy 2:22–23. Discuss a strategy to pursue peace and to avoid disputes.

6. Peace will become ever more accessible as you learn to default to God and His truth in times of uncertainty and stress. Choose a psalm that expresses praise to God for His provision or His deliverance. Read (memorize!) Lamentations 3:22–24. Keep scriptures like these close at hand, either for your own comfort or for handy reference when you're ministering to someone else.

7. Discuss the perks of peace. Which one(s) resonate with you most? Which one(s) draws you to desire more peace in your own life?

TEST YOURSELF ON PEACE

Please READ the following statements and ask yourself, **"Do I agree that this describes me—my thoughts and actions during the last few months?"** Then, CIRCLE a number on the scale (below) from 1 to 10, showing how strongly you disagree or agree that each statement does or does not apply to you. Thus, a "1" means that you totally disagree that this is a strength in your life and a "perfect 10" means that you totally agree that the statement describes one of your strengths.

Totally Disagree	Very Strongly Disagree	Strongly Disagree	Somewhat Disagree	Slightly Disagree	Slightly Agree	Somewhat Agree	Strongly Agree	Very Strongly Agree	Totally Agree
1	2	3	4	5	6	7	8	9	10

1. I am at peace because I know God's plan for my life.	1 2 3 4 5 6 7 8 9 10
2. God gives me a sense of well-being even in hard times.	1 2 3 4 5 6 7 8 9 10
3. I sense God's peacefulness even in hard times.	1 2 3 4 5 6 7 8 9 10
4. I have a quiet confidence around other people.	1 2 3 4 5 6 7 8 9 10
5. I feel God's hand on my life, regardless of setbacks.	1 2 3 4 5 6 7 8 9 10
6. Other people say that they see the peace of God in me.	1 2 3 4 5 6 7 8 9 10
TOTAL SCORE (Read directions) =	

SCORE YOURSELF ON PEACE

Take each of the numbered responses you circled, and add up the numbers to make a total score. For example, if you answered "7" to all 6

questions, the total would be 42. Write the total in the box below the questions, and also mark the location of your score on the chart below:

SCORING CHART FOR PEACE

(Mark a line through the location of your score)

6 10 15 20 **25** 30 **35** 40 41 42 43 44 45 **46** 47 48 49 50 51 52 53 **54** 55 56 57 58 **59** 60

INTERPRETING YOUR SCORE: The middle point (46) represents the average score obtained by typical readers. Below-average scores are 35 or less, and those below 25 are extremely low. Above-average scores are 54 or more, and scores above 59 are extremely high.

If your score is below average, discuss your results with a friend and see if you can identify possible areas of improvement in peace.

Chapter Eight

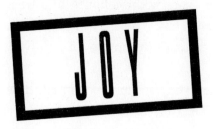

In times of joy, all of us wished we possessed a tail we could wag.

W.H. AUDEN

Joy is the most infallible sign of the presence of God.

PIERRE TEILHARD DE CHARDIN

What picture pops into your mind when you hear the word "joy"?

Some will see Snoopy, dancing on his beagle back feet with great abandon, "arms" thrown wide, ears flying in the wind, feet madly treading air.

Others might remember holding that new grandbaby for the first time, counting those tiny toes and looking for family resemblances.

Some who live in my corner of the country might describe the thrill of rafting the wild white water of the Deschutes River or rappelling down a sheer cliff at Smith Rock.

Winston Churchill had his own perspective on joy, once remarking that "nothing in life is so exhilarating as to be shot at without result."

Obviously joy means very different things to different people!

But tell me this: Would you normally use the term "joy" to describe your emotional state while enduring a savage beating? How about if you were trapped inside your body, confined to a wheelchair, not able to walk, eat, talk, or even take a breath without assistance? Would you be joyful if you found yourself in constant pain or if your very life were in jeopardy?

Believe it or not, you can know joy in all those situations, and in others just as dire. The truth is, you can experience joy when you're not happy at all. Joy is so much more, so much better and longer lasting than happiness.

Happiness is all about the happenings of our lives. It's tied directly to our particular set of circumstances. It is the sunny-day, winning, good-health, fame-and-fortune, here-comes-the-ice-cream-truck feeling. Any of us can be happy when things are going right…but what happens in the face of tragedy, defeat, sorrow, or loss?

That, my friend, is when joy carries the day!

Fleeting and ephemeral as it is, happiness cannot satisfy. Happiness is a will-o'-the-wisp. A puff of vapor. Fickle. The circumstances that bring happiness on one occasion may not achieve the same response in your heart the second time around. Your boyfriend sent you flowers at work? Next time he'd better pick you up for lunch in a limo!

IT'S OKAY TO ENJOY LIFE

God has designed us for joy. A crabby Christian is an oxymoron. Even when we have what seems like more than our share of adversity, God has equipped us to have an optimistic, joyful attitude toward life.

The renowned preacher Charles Spurgeon used to come under censure for having too much fun in life. Numerous critics among his clerical peers felt he was entirely too lighthearted for a man of the cloth. Why, he even allowed humor in the pulpit—sometimes laughing right out loud! When the indignant clergymen finally arranged a meeting to chastise Spurgeon for his irreverence, he replied, "Gentlemen, if you knew how much I hold back, you would commend me!"

Spurgeon simply gave expression to the joy that God has for all of us.

THE INSIDE SMILE

What is joy? Can it really be defined?

I like to think of it as an *inside smile*. It's both a particular feeling occasioned by circumstances and a general approach to life itself. We experience joy as pleasure, delight, inner warmth, cheerfulness, contentment, or excitement. While not perfectly synonymous with any one of those terms, it somehow embraces them all.

A sense of joy can be an abiding assurance or eager expectation of something anticipated, or it can be a response to an event or situation. It may be as simple as suddenly realizing how blessed you are that God loves you, no matter what. As that insight washes over you, a sense of delight and comfort settles in. When you are certain of good things in the future, having confidence that God is bigger than any giant you are facing or could ever face, it gives you the ability to transcend your immediate difficulties, no matter how challenging or painful they are.

We gain joy in any number of ways, but here are a few essential joy-makers.

IT'S A PERK FROM KNOWING GOD

Joy is a gift from God Himself. David remarked, "You have put gladness in my heart.... For You alone, O LORD, make me dwell in safety" (Psalm 4:7–8).

Isn't that good? It is God, and God alone, who places gladness in a human heart.

David, of course, knew God's faithfulness firsthand. When the Lord gave him supernatural victories in battle, or hid him from Saul in the rocks and caves so he wouldn't be apprehended, David knew his reasons for joy came from God alone. His inside smile was not the result of his own strength and cunning.

What peace and joy in the realization that our very lives rest in the palm of a loving Father.

Joy is one of the perks of living inside God's plan—perhaps the most wonderful benefit of all. My own experience testifies to the fact that the more I live my life according to God's purposes, depending on Him for everything, the more joy wells up within, spilling over the walls of my life and washing across my path.

That inside smile is a gift from God Himself.

And there is nothing in the universe quite like it.

IT'S BUILT INTO HIS WORD

When we immerse ourselves in God's Word, we stand in that confident assurance that produces joy. The more we ingest and digest His enduring truth, the more joy we experience. Jeremiah, known as "the weeping prophet," laid his heart bare about the impact of God's word: "Your words were found, and I ate them, and Your word was to me the joy and rejoicing of my heart" (Jeremiah 15:16).

This prophet's life was downright difficult. In fact, it was grueling. But he drank in God's truth—great long draughts of it—and in spite of his tears, in spite of everything, his heart filled with joy.

When John reminded the early church of the incomparable inheritance they had in Christ, the majesty and magnificence of Jesus he had seen in His transfiguration, he said, "And these things we write to you that your joy may be full" (1 John 1:4).

John knew the great truths about God. He had personally lived with

Jesus, had seen Him perform countless miracles, and ate with Him after He had been raised from the dead. He even witnessed Jesus' ascension into heaven. His experience with the Lord was powerful, and he wanted others to know everything the Lord said was true! They could count on it. If they would take in God's truth and trust it, their joy would be full.

And so will ours.

IT GETS BETTER UNDER PRESSURE

Trials, tribulation, attacks, tension, call them what you will—the pressure points in life are some of the best joy makers. How is that possible? James puts it in perspective: "Dear brothers and sisters, *whenever trouble comes your way, let it be an opportunity for joy*. For when your faith is tested, your endurance has a chance to grow. So let it grow, for when your endurance is fully developed, you will be strong in character and ready for anything" (James 1:2–4, NLT, emphasis mine).

The Bible isn't telling us here to love our trials, but rather to appreciate the growth in godly character they produce.

Helen Keller came to understand that personally. Looking back at her own limitations, she wrote, "The marvelous richness of human experience would lose something of rewarding joy if there were no limitations to overcome. The hilltop hour would not be half so wonderful if there were no dark valleys to traverse."

Doesn't the sunshine always feel more intense after the gray rain has dominated the sky for a time?

Charlie Wedemeyer was a football fanatic. He was so gifted at the sport that he became an All-American at Michigan State, launching him into a successful high school coaching career after graduation. He threw himself passionately into making state contenders out of his kids at Los Gatos High School in northern California. Great things lay ahead for him and his wife Lucy.

It was a marvelous life until 1977, when Charlie was diagnosed with ALS (Lou Gehrig's disease). Barely thirty years old, he was given one to three years to live. With its relentless march through his body, the disease slowly removed pieces of the life Charlie had loved. Paralysis began to set in, rendering him unable to walk on his own. But with the same determination that made him an all-star, Charlie had his wife Lucy drive him up and down the sidelines of the games so he could continue coaching.

When the disease robbed him of his ability to speak out loud, Lucy would read his lips and relay his instructions to the team. The disability worsened, but his determination soared.

One to three years has become almost thirty. These days Charlie is able to move only his eyes, eyebrows, and lips. Yet he continues not only to coach but to travel all over the world speaking, with Lucy reading his lips and bringing his words. "I love to give others hope," Charlie says confidently.

When she speaks about their situation, all they have had to endure across the years, Lucy concludes with these remarkable words: "We share our story hoping that you will come to understand the true peace and the love that we have found. This is how we have overcome the obstacles that we face every day and this is how we continue to live life full of hope and full of joy…Some people might view our story as a tragedy, and yet because of our relationship with God, we have found more love and joy in our lives than most healthy people will ever know. By surrendering our lives to God, we have true purpose in our lives… We have more joy in our lives today than we ever had before Charlie's illness."[1]

That, my friend, is supernatural.

As James says, when we look to the Lord in the midst of trials rather than curse the darkness, we experience an inside smile that can only be wrought by Him! He is bigger than any problem we might face, and He will confound the plans of hell by strengthening us through the very trials that seek to destroy us!

IT FLOWS FROM A HEART OF WORSHIP

Worship and joy are reciprocal. They enhance one another. We rejoice in worship, and our joy increases as we extol the virtues of God. When the young King David brought the ark of God into the capital city, he made a point of leading the parade. David celebrated the greatness and majesty of God with such joy that he "danced before the LORD with all his might"! (2 Samuel 6:14). When you're awestruck by the presence of the Lord, it's natural to have a smile on the inside that breaks out on the outside!

Personally I find it odd to consider "stoic praise."

"I'm praising God deep down," someone will say, "you just can't see it. I don't need to get emotional about it."

Well and good, I suppose. And God certainly knows the heart. But just between you and me, I still don't get it. How can a person gather with other believers in the presence of the living God, the Creator of the Universe, and not get a little excited? How can a child of God draw close to the One who formed us and gives us every breath—the One who gave His Son to purchase us from slavery and death and bring us into His very family circle—and respond quietly and passively with no outward expression of joy?

The same individual who sits on his hands on Sunday, superglued to the pew, loses all sense of decorum at the basketball game Friday night—shouting, jumping up and down, and giving high fives to complete strangers! Put this in perspective with me: We're talking about a game that lasts forty-eight minutes versus life that lasts for eternity. Which one should be greeted with a shout of joy?

When you consider who God is and recognize that He gives you an audience every time you worship, you can't help but smile inside. Whatever else might be going on in your life, God is God, and He holds your life in His mighty hand. And now you are in His presence, and He has chosen to be with you and receive your gift of praise. As David said: "You will show me the path of life; in Your presence is fullness of joy; at Your right hand are pleasures forevermore" (Psalm 16:11).

IT BLOSSOMS FROM NEW LIFE

When you study the life of the church that grew up after Jesus ascended into heaven, you are struck by the joy that filled the lives of new converts when they opened their hearts to the Lord.

The book of Acts tells the story of how the Holy Spirit directed Philip to set out down the desolate desert road between Jerusalem and Gaza. The Spirit further instructed him to catch up with an Ethiopian official who was riding in his chariot, reading the prophet Isaiah's words out loud. Seizing the moment for Christ, Philip offered to explain the meaning of the passage that so puzzled the foreign visitor, and the man readily responded by listening and putting his faith in Jesus. The official was so thrilled he asked Philip to baptize him on the spot, symbolizing the beginning of an entirely new life in Christ.

As Philip left that place, the Bible says that the Ethiopian "went on his way rejoicing" (Acts 8:39).

That's the nature of salvation—it fills you with joy. You know God loves you, has forgiven and cleansed you, and set you on a path to an entirely new experience of life. Talk about an inside smile—it threatens to split you apart!

I remember the experience of meeting Jesus as if it were yesterday. The boundless elation I felt as I entered into that new relationship was so all-encompassing I lived in a bubble of joy for months on end. All was right with my world, and I knew it. Did that mean my life became a smooth path through a flower garden? Hardly! What it did mean was that in spite of the challenges I faced in those days, I knew God loved me, was involved in my life from then on, and had great plans for me.

The inside smile from those days has never left!

The benefits that come into our lives with joy are many, varied, remarkable, and as real and solid as the book you hold in your hands. Consider just a few:

- Joy gives us hope. (See Isaiah 55:12; 1 Thessalonians 4:13.)
- Joy gives us strength. (See Nehemiah 8:10–12.)
- Joy gives us rewards. (See 1 Peter 4:13.)
- Joy gives us a victorious perspective on life. (See 2 Corinthians 6:4–10; Philippians 4:4, 13.)

BEWARE OF THE KILLJOYS

Joy is such a significant facet of God's life in Christ, the "Dark Side" makes constant attempts to dilute, steal, or kill your joy altogether. Both the new believer and the seasoned saint need to be on their toes to keep joy breakers at bay! Some of them are easily recognizable, while others are more insidious.

The devil

God's people have an enemy in the spirit world who delights in destroying their joy. Knowing that the joy of the Lord is their strength, he and his minions pull out all the stops to attack the competition. No question, in addition to being the father of lies, he is king of the killjoys!

This is why the Bible reminds us to be vigilant, on our toes, because the devil roams around "like a roaring lion, seeking whom he may devour" (1 Peter 5:8). How encouraging it is to realize that Satan is only a created being whose powers can't even touch the supernatural powers of our Savior! But at the same time, if you fail to take him seriously, the price will be far greater than you'll want to pay.

Guilt from confessed sin

Believers know that "all have sinned and fall short of the glory of God" (Romans 3:23). We have missed the mark of perfection, and when we allow our thoughts to review those past sins—now under the blood of Jesus Christ—we open ourselves to a heaping portion of guilt! The Bible assures us that if we confess our sins, God graciously forgives and cleanses us. Yet we all know how easy it is to rehearse *those things* that we did or said.

While a certain amount of regret over our past failures might be inevitable, it is *essential* for us to focus on God's truth, to stay mindful of His overpowering grace. The Bible says, "As far as the east is from the west, so far has He removed our transgressions from us" (Psalm 103:12). In the book of Jeremiah, our God assures us, "I will forgive their iniquity, and their sin I will remember no more" (31:34).

God's forgiveness is real, and His power is sufficient to cleanse us. Don't allow guilt from already-confessed-forsaken-and-forgiven sins rob you of your joy. Don't let *anything* rob you of your joy!

Be angry, but don't sin

Nothing can quench the flame of joy more quickly than anger. That's why Paul cautions us not to let the sun set on our anger, lest it eat away at our peace and well-being.

I remember the day back in high school chemistry class when we were preparing to do an experiment with sulfuric acid. A friend of mine "borrowed" a pen from a classmate and proceeded to drop it into a test tube of the stuff. In no time at all, the paint peeled off and the acid began to eat away at the plastic itself. Needless to say, the pen had to be replaced!

We forget that's how acid works. Since we can't see the acid produced by anger, we're unaware it's there. Meanwhile it eats away at our insides, stripping us of the joy of life. We need to get on top of anger before it gets on top of us!

Oh, my aching back

It's easy to appreciate how pain can diminish our joy. How can you feel a sense of delight, of confident assurance or expectation, when you're wracked with pain? Having experienced incessant pain myself, I understand how difficult it is to keep it in perspective. That's why I am so thankful for God's truth! I know that "weeping may endure for a night, but joy comes in the morning" (Psalm 30:5). In the midst of the pain, we need to set our eyes on the Prince of Peace, the only One greater than our pain!

Pickle-puss people

As Jesus was on His way to heal a little girl hovering near death, He and the child's father were met by some people with the bad news that she was already dead. There was no need, they insisted, to bother Jesus any further.

Jesus, however, paid no attention to the information—and even forbade those people to follow Him to the child's home. When they got to the house, a wake for the dead daughter had already begun, and those in attendance ridiculed Jesus for saying that the little girl was only sleeping. In response, He put them all out and promptly raised her from the dead!

Not one of those scoffers was allowed to witness one of the Bible's greatest, most joyous miracles. Jesus wasn't interested in pickle-puss people stealing anybody's joy!

If you hang around with chronically negative complainers, they'll do their level best to grab both sides of your inside smile and turn it upside down. Negative people can't stand it when they encounter simple, lighthearted joy. They will go right to work trying to make you as negative, miserable, and joyless as they are! You simply cannot afford to spend your time with such people.

THIS JOY'S FOR YOU!

One of my favorite worship songs from years ago came straight from the book of Isaiah. The music was unremarkable, but the message was so encouraging I never stopped singing it. May it rest in your heart, too: "Therefore the redeemed of the LORD shall return, and come with singing unto Zion, and everlasting joy shall be upon their heads. They shall obtain gladness and joy, and sorrow and mourning shall flee away!" (Isaiah 35:10).

Not to alarm our stoic brethren, but it's enough to make you want to dance. Or even laugh out loud!

◆ POINTS TO PONDER ◆

1. Define *joy* and contrast it with *happiness*, as described in the first part of the chapter. Do you agree with the distinctions that the author drew?

2. Describe a time when you felt joyful and victorious in spite of circumstances.

3. Some of us have temperaments that are more serious than others. Does that mean that we don't experience God's joy?

4. Read Psalm 86:3–4. What does this say about the source of joy? Did you realize that you could make this request of God in this way?

5. Do you have a particular Bible verse that's a joy maker for you? If so, write it down. If not, find one and memorize it!

6. Relate an experience in which adversity strengthened your joy.

7. How does worship enhance joy and joy enhance worship for you?

8. Don't let guilt from confessed sin rob you of your joy. But what about unconfessed sin?

9. What joy killers do you experience from time to time? What do you do to combat their effect?

10. Read and discuss the story of Ahab and Naboth's vineyard in 1 Kings 21:1–16. What personal experience have you had with this powerful joy killer?

TEST YOURSELF ON JOY

Please READ the following statements and ask yourself, **"Do I agree that this describes me—my thoughts and actions during the last few months?"** Then, CIRCLE a number on the scale (below) from 1 to 10, showing how strongly you disagree or agree that each statement does or does not apply to you. Thus, a "1" means that you totally disagree that this is a strength in your life and a "perfect 10" means that you totally agree that the statement describes one of your strengths.

Totally Disagree	Very Strongly Disagree	Strongly Disagree	Somewhat Disagree	Slightly Disagree	Slightly Agree	Somewhat Agree	Strongly Agree	Very Strongly Agree	Totally Agree
1	2	3	4	5	6	7	8	9	10

1. I continually have an inner quiet and joy about my future.	1 2 3 4 5 6 7 8 9 10
2. God gives me a feeling of joy regardless of the cares of life.	1 2 3 4 5 6 7 8 9 10
3. I am a very joyful person around other people.	1 2 3 4 5 6 7 8 9 10
4. I often feel a deep joy even when times are hard.	1 2 3 4 5 6 7 8 9 10
5. I feel joyful when I know I'm doing God's work.	1 2 3 4 5 6 7 8 9 10
6. Other people say that they see godly joy in me.	1 2 3 4 5 6 7 8 9 10
TOTAL SCORE (Read directions) =	

SCORE YOURSELF ON JOY

Take each of the numbered responses you circled, and add up the numbers to make a total score. For example, if you answered "6" to all 6

questions, the total would be 36. Write the total in the box below the questions, and also mark the location of your score on the chart below:

SCORING CHART FOR JOY

(Mark a line through the location of your score)

6 10 15 20 **25** 30 **35** 40 41 42 43 44 45 **46** 47 48 49 50 51 52 53 **54** 55 56 57 58 **59** 60

INTERPRETING YOUR SCORE: The middle point (46) represents the average score obtained by typical readers. Below-average scores are 35 or less, and those below 25 are extremely low. Above-average scores are 54 or more, and scores above 59 are extremely high.

If your score is below average, discuss your results with a friend and see if you can identify possible areas of improvement in joy.

Chapter Nine

The ship that will not obey the helm
will have to obey the rocks.

ENGLISH PROVERB

If you keep My commandments, you will abide in My love,
just as I have kept My Father's commandments and abide in His love.

JESUS

Words are endlessly fascinating.

They have by-the-book dictionary definitions, but they also elicit *feelings* in us associated with our experiences. Words have shape and texture because of what we bring to them.

Some words are warm. Inviting and embracing. Conjuring up happy and positive images. "Kitty" and "puppy" are warm words, whereas "cat" and "dog" may not be at all.

For me the word "woodstove" is warm—not because of its temperature, but because of the experiences I've had with woodstoves throughout my life. When I hear "woodstove," I immediately think of arriving home on a cold, rainy evening after a long day. The fire crackling in the stove welcomes and comforts me, enveloping me like a cozy blanket. In fact, I want to sit right down with a warm cup of tea and have a chat!

"Woodstove" might not be so pleasant for the one who only recalls hauling and splitting wood, picking up debris off the carpet, or cleaning out the cold, gray ashes. Although you wouldn't find any of those ideas in a dictionary definition, the connotation is clearly there for the person who has had the experiences.

OBEDIENCE—THAT'S COLD!

"Obedience" is almost universally a "cold" word. Negative ideas come to mind when you hear it. You think of…

…a drill sergeant with bulging veins screaming in your face.

…a parent delivering an ultimatum to clean up your room "or else."

…a judge frowning as you try to justify doing 35 mph in a school zone.

…an angry voice barking, "If I've told you once, I've told you a thousand times…."

It seems impossible to think of obedience apart from thoughts of duty, necessity, and compulsion. If you aren't obedient, if you don't do what you're asked, there'll be trouble in River City!

Even in relationship to God, the term "obedience" is distasteful. How can a *commandment* be inviting? Yet as we work to distance ourselves from obedience, we do so to our own great hurt and detriment.

Humanity has wrestled with obedience since the first man drew his first breath on a freshly made, just-out-of-the-box planet. Remember God's commandment to Adam in the Garden? "Of every tree of the garden you may freely eat; but of the tree of the knowledge of good and evil you shall not eat, for in the day that you eat of it you shall surely die" (Genesis 2:16–17).

It was clear as clear. A straightforward command requiring simple obedience. Adam, of course, had more trees than he could count, and they bore bumper crops of luscious fruit. But which one did he choose? The only one that was forbidden. And from that point on, disobedience has been basic to man's makeup, as fundamental as breathing.

Disobedience is a monumental problem—arguably the greatest problem in the universe. Even so, our even greater God has laid out a solution so His people can experience all the good things He has planned and designed for them. The first step in grasping the solution is understanding the true meaning of obedience, as explained in the Manufacturer's instruction book.

WHEN ALL ELSE FAILS...

In order to understand obedience from God's perspective, you need to delete your present understanding of the term and dig afresh into the Bible. The definition of obedience you find in those pages is neither cold nor undesirable. It's warm. Inviting. Alive. The very foundation of a rich and vital relationship with the Creator and Lover of your soul!

In the English language, obedience has little to do with love and a lot to do with law. In the Bible, it's the other way around. While the English term suggests unquestioned authority and militaristic compliance, the Bible gives it a different slant. In Hebrew and Greek, the basic languages of the Bible, obedience does not mean blindly following orders.

No, obedience in the Bible is all about *relationship*.

In the Old Testament, the word normally translated "obedience" comes from a root meaning "to hear, to listen to." It presupposes a relationship based on trust and respect. Because of that relationship, a person listens to what is said or asked and responds accordingly. There is a direct connection between hearing and responding, listening and doing.

A good biblical example of this appears in Deuteronomy 6:4–5: "Hear, O Israel: The LORD our God, the LORD is one! You shall love the

LORD your God with all your heart, with all your soul, and with all your strength."

God had miraculously saved His people from captivity and promised them a glorious new future in a land of their own. All He asked of them was that they would return His love with true, uncompromising devotion. They first needed to hear. Then they needed to respond in obedience.

From God's perspective, that's what obedience is all about. It signifies a response within a relationship rather than a reaction to a rule. God's commandments are not demands for His people to toe the line; they are requests for His people to recognize and reflect the love He has shown to them.

In the New Testament, Jesus lived out this understanding of obedience in the way He responded to His Father. The night before He went to the cross Jesus prayed, "You loved Me before the foundation of the world" (John 17:24). That loving relationship was the basis for the obedience in His life. That's why He later prayed in the Garden of Gethsemane, "Nevertheless not My will, but Yours, be done" (Luke 22:42).

With Jesus, it's impossible to separate obedience from relationship.

IF...THEN

Loving obedience also marks Jesus' followers. He says, "If you love Me, keep My commandments. [Be obedient!].... He who has My commandments and keeps them, it is he who loves Me. And he who loves Me will be loved by My Father, and I will love him and manifest Myself to him" (John 14:15, 21).

Those who follow Jesus do what He desires.

Why? For the simple reason that they're caught up in His love. They know how much He loves them, and they want to do the things that bless Him and please Him—not because they have to, but because they "love to." It's what John highlights when he says, "We love Him because He first loved us" (1 John 4:19). That's why we obey Him!

When you respect and appreciate one in authority over you, you listen to what he says. You do what you can to fulfill any request because you care for that person, and you know he wouldn't be asking you to do something that would be hurtful.

We've learned about this since childhood. When our parents or caregiver told us not to touch a hot burner, we came to understand they did it out of love, to keep us from hurting ourselves. I'll grant you, we probably reacted out of fear of a spanking, but as we grew up, we realized our parents required obedience because of their love for us.

That's what led them to demand that we not play in the street, that we drive carefully, and that we tell them the details of our plans before leaving home. It seemed ridiculously restrictive, but the requests were motivated by love, and the relationship we had with them enabled us to respond obediently.

The heart of obedience is love, not law. What is true in human relationships is also true for the way we relate to God. As we hear God's heart and understand His character, we know He has only our best interests at heart. He doesn't want to use us, He wants to bless us, and enable us to experience everything we were designed for. In our desire to return His love, we trust Him and respond in obedience.

The psalmist writes: "You are good, and do good.... The law of Your mouth is better to me than thousands of coins of gold and silver" (Psalm 119: 68, 72). Understood this way, obedience carries a positive meaning. It's something we "love" to do.

BUT WHAT ABOUT HITLER?

Whenever you talk positively about obeying authority, invariably someone brings up the devastation resulting from blind obedience to powerful people with malevolent agendas. History has paraded authority figures past us like Hitler, Nero, Jim Jones, and Charles Manson, all of whom used their power to perpetrate unimaginable evil. Isn't that one reason we should view "obedience" with a jaundiced eye? Isn't that why the word has acquired such negative connotations?

It all depends on whose authority you're talking about.

Where is this leader taking you? If his or her motives and agenda line up with God's values, there's no problem. When they don't, that's when your obedience to a Greater Authority must take precedence over the lesser one.

A friend of mine was a successful car salesman at a dealership in his community. After he had worked there for some time, the management called him in and told him he needed to change the way he dealt with his customers. Even though the things they asked him to do were by no means uncommon in the industry, they were dishonest.

To be blunt, he was asked to manipulate and lie.

So he faced a big problem.

My friend could blindly obey those in authority over him, or he could rebel against their authority, and disobey them behind their backs. He did neither. He decided to quit the company and get another job! He followed the principle set forth by the apostle Peter: "We ought to obey God rather than men" (Acts 5:29). Obedience to godly principles means you choose to submit only to those authorities whose requests line up with godly values.

If those in authority over us are living lives that reflect God's truth, our obedience will accomplish God's best (Romans 13:1–3). It's only when man's requests come in conflict with God's rules that we need to step back and rethink our allegiances.

THE DOWNSIDE OF DISOBEDIENCE

Question Authority.

You've seen the bumper sticker. It's been around since the sixties—that turbulent and bewildering decade when disobedience became the order of the day. At that time, civil disobedience in some quarters of our land brought about long-awaited justice and equality for African Americans. Because of that particular situation, such "disobedience" came to be regarded as good and useful.

Since then, people in an endless smorgasbord of situations have determined they are above authority or are authorities unto themselves. Nobody can tell them what to do because they have determined they are free to redefine the rules to fit their personal desires.

As a result, among many other examples, we find terrorists masquerading as ecological saviors, burning buildings and vandalizing logging operations in the name of saving trees. Not only is it illogical and immoral, it's illegal! But that's only if you recognize the civilly instituted authority. When you have determined you are the authority yourself, who cares?

Even in government, various branches, commissions, and individuals are publicly seizing authority that is not theirs to advance their private agendas. They ignore existing laws or declare others null and void with impunity.

And there are consequences.

Of course there are.

Disobedience *goes* someplace.

It has real outcomes that God Himself built into the fabric of the universe. Those who choose to disobey will experience the consequences whether they like it or not, believe it or not, trust God or not. It's a part of the package called "Life."

The Bible clearly declares the downside of disobedience—and does not stutter. Just reading what God says in portions of Leviticus 26 sends chills up your spine: "If you do not obey Me, and do not observe all these commandments...or if your soul abhors My judgments...I also will do this to you: I will even appoint terror over you.... You shall sow your seed in vain.... I will break the pride of your power.... Your strength shall be spent in vain..." (vv. 14–16, 19–20) and on it goes. Not a very pretty picture!

We've all had a taste of how this works. Let's say we choose not to believe what God has to say about forgiveness. His Word tells us to let go of the emotional baggage we drag around from an offense committed against us. When we obey Him and forgive, we are set free from our bitterness. But if we disobey and hold bitterness and unforgiveness in our hearts, we pay a price. We risk lowering our immune systems, increasing our risk of cancer, and generally darkening our outlook on life.

Is disobedience worth it?

Consider disobedience in the context of our everyday lives, where we are obligated to obey civil law. Let's say we're late for a meeting, so we drive at 50 mph through a school zone clearly marked "20 mph." Suddenly, a child steps out from behind a car, and we can't stop quickly enough. Lives are irrevocably changed in the blink of an eye, all because of disobedience.

Is it worth it?

In society today we all pay the price for rejecting God's values. As disobedience becomes more common, we edge closer and closer to anarchy. To understand where this ends up, we need only look at the nation of ancient Israel. When they rejected God's laws, desecrated His temple, and turned a deaf ear to His prophets, the society completely fell apart and was overrun by its enemies. Instead of God's people getting what they wanted, they lost what they once had.

Was disobedience worth it? Is it worth it today in our own nation?

It may be that you are new to faith in Christ. If so, continue to remind yourself that you have confessed your sin, and God has truly forgiven, cleansed, and set you free. You must depend on the Lord in the present to be free from the bondage of your past and enter into the new future that He offers you.

On the other hand, if you have been living with the Lord for some time, you will want to broaden your base of dependence. That means depending on Him in areas where you haven't been looking to Him, like making decisions in your business or deciding how to counsel the friend who has a crumbling marriage.

The truth is, you might not even be aware of how much of your life is on autopilot because God has gifted you with great natural abilities and intellect. Ask Him to show you where He would like to give you input.

In the end, dependence is dependence.

If you're going to depend on God for anything, you need to depend on Him for everything. If you are going to be obedient, dependence on God is essential.

Listen to the Lord

Work on listening to the Lord so you can hear His heart for your life. Remember, obedience is about relationship, not rules. That means hearing and responding. God speaks in numerous ways, but one of the most prominent and powerful ways is by means of His Word.

The Bible is a wonderful window to the heart of God. As you read it, you discover that His desires for your life are no deep, dark secret. He reveals His principles of joy, peace, security, stability, and significance—principles the world apart from God can't understand or access because it doesn't know the Author.

To listen to the Lord demands spending time with Him, especially time alone. One of the remarkable things about the life of Jesus was the

HOW DO WE BECOME OBEDIENT?

There is a Grand Designer with a Great Design for the life of e\
son on the planet. God wants to give life, abundant and etern
who trust His only Son Jesus to forgive their sins. That is the ac
dience that initiates and empowers all other obedience throug|
There are still moment-by-moment, day-by-day choices to m
they will be made in light of respect for the character, pov
authority of God.

Live in God's Love

God loves you so much He sent His only Son for you, to {
the means to experience life to its fullest here and now, and in<
able joy in heaven when your life here comes to a close. As you I
day in the reality of God's love, you will desire to obey Him
Word, because you will know He wants His best for you.

When you live in God's love, you'll wrestle less with obedier
God who created you, saved you, gifted and called you thin
good thoughts for you. You begin cultivating obedience by refle<
God's love for you and the innumerable ways He's shown it.

Deepen Your Dependence

Deepen your dependence on the Lord in every area of yc
Start relying on Him for more things, the "Lord, help me find a {
things, the "Lord, I need Your wisdom and strength to discipl
eight-year-old" things, and the "God, please help me love my n
coworker" things.

As you depend more and more (and more and more) on th<
you will discover the good things He has in store for you—u<
ping gift after precious gift—which will increase your trust
faithfulness.

fact that He regularly sought time alone with the Father. If it was important for Him, doesn't it stand to reason it ought to be for us, too? It is in those alone times, chatting with Him while driving, seeking Him late in the evening right before bed, or taking a walk with Him, that there is time to speak to Him and to hear from Him. As we listen, like Solomon said, He will speak: "Hear, my son, and be wise; and guide your heart in the way" (Proverbs 23:19).

Follow Where He Leads

Finally, obedience demands following where God leads you. You respond to what you hear Him saying, and put into practice the principles He gives you. Even when you aren't entirely certain where He's taking you, you obey, because you know He loves you and is committed to you. You follow where He leads.

Will the route God takes you on be easy and free from problems and pain? Definitely not. Men and women in the Bible who followed the Lord didn't live on easy street, but they definitely found the satisfaction they were seeking. When Stephen, the first martyr of the Christian faith, was enduring a mock trial similar to that of Jesus, he looked confidently into heaven and said, "Look! I see the heavens opened and the Son of Man standing at the right hand of God!" As he was being stoned to death, he asked God to forgive his attackers. Wow! What incredible dependence, trust, and willingness to follow the Lord, even to death!

THE UPSIDE OF OBEDIENCE

Innumerable benefits of obedience can be found in every area of our lives. We find the upside of obedience in the same chapter of the Bible that details the downside. And the Up is every bit as Up as the Down is Down.

If you walk in My statutes and keep My commandments and perform them [read that, "exercise obedience"] then I will give you the rain in its season, the land shall yield its produce.... You shall eat your bread to the full, and dwell in your land safely, I will give peace in the land, and you shall lie down, and none will make you afraid.... I will look on you favorably and make you fruitful. (Leviticus 26:3–6, 9)

In other words, obey the Lord and enjoy a life that is rich and full. We will live with the peace of knowing we are right where we're supposed to be, doing just what we've been asked to do, experiencing the satisfaction and fulfillment we seek.

Apart from obedience, it's impossible.

Because of obedience, it's reality.

The Bible begins and ends with obedience. It begins with God expressing His desire for Adam in the Garden and ends by stating, "Blessed are those who do His commandments, that they may have the right to the tree of life, and may enter through the gates into the city" (Revelation 22:14). If God chose to begin and end His Word with obedience, it must be foundational for a successful life. There's an old hymn that sums this up so well:

When we walk with the Lord in the light of His Word,
*   what a glory He sheds on our way!*
While we do His good will, He abides with us still,
*   and with all who will trust and obey.*
Trust and obey, for there's no other way to be happy in Jesus,
*   but to trust and obey.*
Then in fellowship sweet we will sit at His feet
*   or we'll walk by His side in the way.*
What He says, we will do, where He sends, we will go,
*   never fear, only trust and obey.*

◆ POINTS TO PONDER ◆

1. Is "obedience" a warm or cold word to you? What experiences come to mind when you think about obedience?

2. Have you ever thought of Jesus as obedient? Read Philippians 2:5–8. Compare your own experiences with obedience to that of Jesus.

3. What is it about some people that makes them easy or hard to obey? If you are in authority over anyone (parent, employer, manager, civil authority), do people respond well to you? If not, what could you do to change that?

4. Have you ever had to choose between man's authority and God's? What happened?

5. Describe your own disobedience in relationship to civil laws, family relationships, and God's Word. What was achieved or what were the consequences? Have you continued that behavior?

6. Do you live in God's love? Have you embraced the love and life that God wants to give you? Has your understanding of God's love for you increased with time?

7. How would you rate the depth of your dependence on God, 1–10? How would you rate the breadth of your dependence on God, 1–10? Name an area of your life that you handle all by yourself. How could you begin to get God's perspective on that area?

8. When do you regularly listen for God's voice? Do you have a confident expectation that you can hear from Him? Read John 10:27–30. How has God blessed you because you have followed in obedience?

TEST YOURSELF ON OBEDIENCE

Please READ the following statements and ask yourself, **"Do I agree that this describes me—my thoughts and actions during the last few months?"** Then, CIRCLE a number on the scale (below) from 1 to 10, showing how strongly you disagree or agree that each statement does or does not apply to you. Thus, a "1" means that you totally disagree that this is a strength in your life and a "perfect 10" means that you totally agree that the statement describes one of your strengths.

Totally Disagree	Very Strongly Disagree	Strongly Disagree	Somewhat Disagree	Slightly Disagree	Slightly Agree	Somewhat Agree	Strongly Agree	Very Strongly Agree	Totally Agree
1	2	3	4	5	6	7	8	9	10

1. I totally yield to God, being eager to obey.	1 2 3 4 5 6 7 8 9 10
2. God gives me strength to submit to his purposes and timing.	1 2 3 4 5 6 7 8 9 10
3. I obey the Word because my heart wants to serve the Lord.	1 2 3 4 5 6 7 8 9 10
4. I am a very obedient person around people in authority.	1 2 3 4 5 6 7 8 9 10
5. I follow the example of Jesus who obeyed the Father.	1 2 3 4 5 6 7 8 9 10
6. I can easily obey requirements at school or work.	1 2 3 4 5 6 7 8 9 10
TOTAL SCORE (Read directions) =	

SCORE YOURSELF ON OBEDIENCE

Take each of the numbered responses you circled, and add up the numbers to make a total score. For example, if you answered "6" to all 6

questions, the total would be 36. Write the total in the box below the questions, and also mark the location of your score on the chart below:

SCORING CHART FOR OBEDIENCE

(Mark a line through the location of your score)

6 10 15 20 25 **30** 35 **40** 41 42 43 44 45 **46** 47 48 49 50 51 52 53 **54** 55 56 57 58 **59** 60

INTERPRETING YOUR SCORE: The middle point (46) represents the average score obtained by typical readers. Below-average scores are 40 or less, and those below 30 are extremely low. Above-average scores are 54 or more, and scores above 59 are extremely high.

If your score is below average, discuss your results with a friend and see if you can identify possible areas of improvement in obedience.

Chapter Ten

It is better to be faithful than famous.

THEODORE ROOSEVELT

Now I saw heaven opened, and behold, a white horse.
And He who sat on him was called Faithful and True.

REVELATION 19:11

Old Faithful.

This popular and famous geyser has become all but synonymous with Yellowstone National Park. Thrusting thousands of gallons of boiling water over 100 feet into the air, she commands a place on most park visitors' must-see list.

But what makes this geyser such a compelling attraction? Other geysers spout higher, with greater volume of water. Besides these, tourists can fill their eyes with the wonder of Yellowstone Falls, catch sight of plentiful wildlife, or wander past boiling mud cauldrons and fascinating geothermal phenomena in the park. So what's the big thing about this one particular geyser? What's her claim to fame?

She's faithful.

She can be counted on to produce what she promises time after time.

Would that people were as faithful as this geyser! Unfortunately, they are far less dependable and trustworthy—and have been since the dawn of civilization. That's probably what moved the writer of Proverbs to state, *"Who can find a faithful man?"*

I can't help wondering what Solomon would say about men and women in twenty-first-century America. Are faithful people easier to locate today than they were in ancient Israel?

Sadly, that isn't the case at all.

THE WAY WE WERE

My dad was born in the early twentieth century. His approach to life was simple, straightforward, and as consistent as Old Faithful. The years came and went, but Dad's way of walking through life didn't really change much. Even as the values and practices in the world around him changed dramatically, Dad continued to function the way he always had.

When he bid a refrigeration job, he determined a fair price, offered the bid, and usually made a verbal agreement with his customer right on the spot. There were no contracts, no legally binding documents between him and the people he knew and trusted. Rarely did anyone try to weasel out of an agreement; rarely did anyone claim that the agreed-upon price was misremembered.

On my dad's side of things, there was no question about keeping his commitment. He would never break that trust. Never. His word was his bond. When he said he was going to do a job for a specific amount, that's what he did, even if he lost money due to an oversight in his bid. Even when a customer deliberately took advantage of him, that didn't change the way Dad did business. He said what he meant and meant what he said. He could be counted on. He was faithful.

Dad's story sounds rather unique these days. But here's my point: *In his era, it wasn't unique at all.* It was repeated many times over in the lives of men and women across this country. Subsequent generations, however, haven't fostered those values—and our society has radically changed.

Faithfulness is no longer an expectation, let alone a requirement for successful business dealings. On the contrary, we now assume people are *not* trustworthy. That we'll have to hold their feet to the fire. That if there's a way out of their commitment, they'll find it, and if none exists, they'll create it. We see it everywhere, don't we?

Consider professional sports. This is going to date me, but I remember the days when teams were committed to one another for the long haul. It would have been inconceivable for Pee Wee Reese to walk away from Duke Snider and the Dodgers, just as Joe DiMaggio never would have turned his back on Phil Rizzuto and the Yankees. Unthinkable! The idea would never have made it to first base.

THE WAY WE ARE

Contrast that with what we find today: Bonds of loyalty and commitment have virtually disappeared from sports. Professional sports teams are little more than revolving doors. Players leave teams regularly when offered higher salaries, and teams trade hometown heroes to put themselves in a better position to win a championship.

Immediately after winning the pennant that had eluded the Red Sox for eighty years, thirteen members of the championship team filed for free agency, testing the waters to see if they could get better contracts elsewhere. In no time at all, the team that *won* was the team that *was.* Who were those players concerned about? Their city? Their longsuffering fans? Their teammates? The Boston kids who revered and idolized them? The future of their team?

Are you kidding? The only thing that mattered was how many millions they could stuff in their back pockets.

Faithfulness, commitment, loyalty, dependability—call it what you will—it's definitely evaporating from our twenty-first-century culture.

Ponder for a moment what has happened to marriage. Again harkening back to my youth, virtually all of my friends grew up with the same set of biological parents. It didn't mean they all had great family lives. Every home wasn't like Ozzie and Harriet's or the Huxtables's. But it did mean that you could bank on families staying together. Divorced parents or kids living in blended families were rare exceptions, not the assumed rule.

Not so in today's society.

It seems more common than not for children and teens now to have a different last name than their parents. Why? They carry the name of their dad who is no longer married to their mom, a woman who has long since remarried, perhaps more than once. What has happened? Without a doubt, it has everything to do with this critical character quality called faithfulness.

WHERE ARE THE PROMISES?

I've been performing weddings now for thirty-five years. While there are several versions of the wedding vows, at the heart of them all, two people promise before God to be committed to one another for life.

That's the long and the short of it.

It is a permanent sealing of two lives.

The bride and groom state clearly for everyone to hear that they are entering into a completely new relationship. They promise to take one another "for better for worse, for richer for poorer, in sickness and in health, to love and to cherish *till death do us part.*"

I have never known this vow to be stated with a nod and a wink. I have never seen bride or groom cross their fingers behind their backs, rendering the declarations null and void. In every wedding I've ever performed, the promises have been freely made before God and people—life commitments given and received. Never has there been a hint of an expectation that sooner or later all will dissolve because of the possibility of "a better deal."

Even so, it happens.

Solemn promises and commitments before God and man are tossed like yesterday's coffee grounds. Sadly, society has begun to regard marriage like acquiring a car. When the new ride turns heads because it's shiny and fun and—well—*new*, that's great! But there comes a time when "the old gray mare, she ain't what she used to be," and she needs to be replaced with a newer model, with more "happening" lines and color, with less upkeep. Surely that perfect set of wheels is out there to replace the old clunker.

Much as we'd like to think otherwise, trading in a marriage is an infinitely more serious matter than replacing a used car. There is a human dimension, both emotional and spiritual, that makes it entirely different. In marriage two people become one, truly and literally "joined together" before the watching eyes of heaven.

When that union is ripped apart—for *whatever* reason—the emotional consequences are staggering. Incalculable. The turmoil, uncertainty, sense of failure, anger, and fear of the future that result from the demise of a marriage are devastating, and children of divorced parents struggle the rest of their lives with issues of faithfulness. They may have no faith at all in anything or anybody, or they may struggle with commitment themselves. Not a very pretty picture!

Whatever happened to faithfulness? Why is it so difficult for us as a society to address the core issue of commitment and loyalty? Is this a virus mutating so rapidly it's impossible to find a cure?

Regardless of the venue—whether we're talking about professional sports, marriage, or relationships within the church—we find the same problem rearing its ugly head: We are unfaithful, uncommitted people.

We simply cannot be counted on for the long haul. When we have an abrasive disagreement with a neighbor, we find it easier to move than to resolve the conflict. If we are at odds with the coach, we try to get him fired or we quit the team. And when we don't agree with an important decision at church? Surely there's a perfect church down the street!

Has faithfulness honestly disappeared completely? Must the answer to Solomon's question be as elusive for us as it was for him?

DESIRE ISN'T ENOUGH

Knowing what we know about our unfaithfulness, it's a somewhat curious thing that a breach of faith still catches us by surprise. That's why we experience such distress when we think someone is being untruthful, or when we find that a spouse or friend has violated our trust. Certainly "unfaithfulness" has been the ruin of many a marriage. Why? Because we all assume that our spouse will be faithful to the wedding vows.

We carry this assumption into all our interactions. How could life go forward if we didn't?

- When we put money in the bank, we expect it to appear in our account. We presume the teller will account for it accurately.
- When we cast our vote, we expect it to be counted and added to the column of our candidate of choice.
- When we leave our car with the mechanic to be repaired, we expect it to be fixed, and also assume we will be charged for work actually done, nothing more and nothing less.

Isn't that right? We expect integrity in day-to-day interactions with people in our community. Yet time and again we find ourselves let down.

Obviously, desiring it is not the same thing as experiencing it. Where is faithfulness?

ONE WHO IS FAITHFUL

What a breath of fresh air it is to experience the faithfulness of God!

He is the headwater of faithfulness.

It is His nature, His practice, His reputation. His promise.

Unlike what we deal with every day, in Him we find One who is always faithful, always keeps His word, and who can always be counted on to deliver what He declares. The Lord God is the original Promise Keeper.

Faithfulness is so basic to God's being that it's impossible to understand Him apart from it. From cover to cover in the Bible we see that He is worthy of our trust and faith.

Noah experienced God's faithfulness. When all mankind had turned its back on God, and the evil of the world had pushed Him to the limit, God decided to destroy the world and everything in it. But there was something about Noah that made Him change His mind.

As a result, He struck a deal with Noah.

If Noah would build a boat longer than a football field and load it up with a pair of every living thing on the earth, God would save him, his wife, his three sons, and their wives when He destroyed everything with a great flood.

Now we're talking trust! Noah had never seen rain. What was a flood? If he could ever finish the monster-sized vessel, how was he supposed to get all the animals into it? And how could he begin to gather enough food to satisfy them all? We don't know what went through his mind; we only know that Noah obeyed. He followed God's instructions to the letter, and God produced what He had promised. He saved Noah and his entourage from the flood, and used them to reestablish life on the earth.

From the day Noah stepped off the ark, a rainbow arch in the heavens reminded him—and reminds all of us—of God's faithfulness to His promises.

FAITHFULNESS CAN BE A REALITY

As God is faithful, He desires that His people reflect that faithfulness as well. When they do, they communicate His character accurately. His will is that we are faithful both to Him and to one another.

Faithfulness to God and faithfulness to people look different from one another. To be faithful to God is to be so full of faith in Him (faithfull) that we trust Him implicitly. We believe we can count on Him, depend on Him to keep His word. We believe that His written Word can be trusted, that we can rely on the truths presented in the Bible, even when we don't understand them or they seem wildly at odds with contemporary culture. As we study His Word, He addresses every significant issue we face. When we follow it from principle to practice, we see why He is so trustworthy: it all makes good sense!

To be faithful to man, then, is to reflect God's faithfulness to us in our relationship with others.

As God can be trusted, so can we.

As He is reliable, so are we.

As He can be taken at His Word, so can we.

As Jesus encourages us, our yes is a *yes*, and our no a *no*. We are faithful to Him as we are faithful to one another. We then see this faithfulness hard at work in every area of our lives.

TILL DEATH DO US PART

Consider the issue of marriage. We live in a society where divorce is at least as common as matrimony. Divorce among those who claim to be no choice. If God is trustworthy and the Bible is the truth, His way is the only way, and His way is faithfulness.

Being faithful to God means being faithful to mirror His faithfulness. Just as He is faithful to us, so we are faithful to one another, trustworthy, reliable, able to be taken at our word.

This is so often where we find ourselves navigating choppy waters. With continual pressure to compromise our commitments and relax our standards, it sometimes seems impossible to maintain the standard of faithfulness. After all, a person can only swim upstream so long.

That's why it's so encouraging to realize that when we have a personal relationship with God, He gives us both the pattern for faithfulness and the wherewithal to make it a personal reality. The point? We don't have to do it on our own!

AS A MAN THINKS IN HIS HEART, SO HE IS

If we are going to be faithful ourselves, it's critical to fill our minds with images of faithfulness. That way, instead of allowing the world to press us into its mold of unfaithfulness, we can focus on examples of faithfulness and model our lives accordingly. Certainly the Bible is full of these word pictures. But we can find them around us in everyday life as well.

As a young college student, it was my privilege to have a professor who taught me the meaning of faithfulness without ever saying a word. Dr. Norman Huffman was a Bible scholar, one of the translators of an early "contemporary" version of the Bible. The picture he painted with his life was so powerful words weren't necessary.

In one of the first class meetings of a new semester, I was seated in the classroom with the rest of the students waiting for the professor to arrive. We all glanced up when Dr. Huffman appeared in the doorway with a lady on his arm. It quickly became apparent she needed some assistance, but he escorted her with a dignity befitting royalty. When

Christians appears to be as frequent as among those who have no
at all. Yet in the Bible, clearly God is not supportive of divorce.

While it can be argued that there are times and situation
demand a parting of the ways, God holds up the standard of ma
that lasts. In very practical terms, that means that when we hit a
spot in our marriage, the "d" word doesn't slip through our l
doesn't even pop into our minds, because we have made a commi
to one another before God and our friends that we are in it to wi
we are dedicated to one another for the long haul.

Though there may be times when we need help from other l
ers and sisters to see the bigger picture or find a better way to
through the relationship jungle we find ourselves in, we can be co
on not to bolt and run or check out emotionally. As we then
through those tough patches that seem to show up in every mai
we find ourselves growing in strength and maturity.

Faithfulness does that. It grows us up and makes us stronge
much more, our long-standing commitment to one another speak
umes to the children we rear. Without saying a word about i
enduring commitment to each other teaches invaluable lessons.

Though we often fail to consider it, as we are faithful to one ar
in our marriages, we give an accurate representation of the charac
God Himself. Just as He remains faithful to us no matter what, j
He keeps His word and stands by His promises, we do the same
each other. What a statement that makes to a world filled with b
relationships!

PLAN TO SWIM UPSTREAM

To be faithful to God at times means going against the current o
temporary culture. Yet if we are truly faithful to God, believin
Word to be the unquestionable standard for our lives, then there's

she was comfortably situated in the back of the room, he strode to the front and began his lecture.

When class ended, before any of us even stood up, he escorted her out of the room and back to his office.

We were all mystified and touched by this display of extreme gentility and respect, and found out later that the lady was the professor's wife. She had been injured in a car accident while studying in Italy on a Fulbright scholarship soon after they were married. In that split-second impact on an Italian highway, both their lives and futures were irreversibly altered.

Now consider Dr. Huffman's situation, especially in light of the way we live today. He was a young man, with his entire professional career ahead of him, who potentially would need to become the full-time care-taker of his wife. Why would he, why should he remain in that relationship? Wouldn't it be better for everybody involved to put his wife in a place where she could receive around-the-clock care by trained professionals?

Dr. Huffman, however, had made a vow to God and to his wife that he was committed to her for the long haul, for better or worse, richer or poorer, in sickness and in health. When he ended up with "worse, poorer, and sickness," he was still committed.

100 percent.

Why?

Because he was faithful.

In addition to the great stories of faithfulness in the Bible, how help-ful it is to carry pictures in your mind to help you know how it looks when it hits the street.

FIRST STEPS

No doubt tackling one issue at a time in your life is also a way to culti-vate faithfulness. If you struggle with tardiness, then don't allow yourself the luxury of being "fashionably late" any longer. See what it's like to be the first one into the office in the morning, or arrive at church thirty minutes early and shock everybody!

Perhaps keeping your word to your kids is a weakness. After all, they're just kids. They won't think much about it if you don't follow through. Or will they? How hard would it be, if you were to announce that next summer you were going to visit Disneyland, to start a savings account at the same time just for that purpose? Think about how much fun it would be for the whole family to select a hotel, then go online and actually make the reservation. What a way to put capital in your "promise keeper" account!

Determine that you will stop stretching the truth, or start being the same person at work on Tuesday that you were at church on Sunday. Pay attention to what you commit to. There are a million "little things" you can do to establish a pattern of faithfulness in your life. Without question, they all add up. Figure out what changes need to be made, and go to work on them! If there's a particularly difficult area, find a trusted friend to hold you accountable.

DON'T SET YOURSELF UP FOR FAILURE

A key factor in developing faithfulness is avoiding situations that engender unfaithfulness. How many times do married people spend their recreational time with friends who are single? How will that work to strengthen their marriage? Or how about the individuals who give themselves permission to peruse pornography on their computers? How destructive will that be in their marriage? Is it a good idea when you're married to have lunch alone with a person of the opposite sex who is not your spouse?

Early in my ministry I got a phone call one morning from a frantic woman who "had to see me." Long before we were attuned to spousal abuse, she experienced it in an up-close-and-personal way. Just the night before her husband had chosen to use her as a punching bag, and she was in a world of hurt. She was calling me from work and wondered if I could meet her during her lunch hour. Of course I agreed, selecting a popular restaurant close to her place of employment.

When she walked in, she was wearing sunglasses to hide the bruise she had on one of her eyes. Although she had done her best to conceal it with makeup, knowing what I knew, it wasn't hard to see what had happened. We were seated, ordered our lunches, and talked about her situation. In less than an hour's time, we were able to accomplish some things that would help her at least short-term.

We prayed together there at our table, and I bid her farewell at the door. "Wow," I thought to myself, "that was really a great counseling opportunity!"

As I was on my way back to the office, it hit me.

What if somebody recognized me at that restaurant and made some invalid assumptions about why I was with the lady? For that matter, why hadn't I figured out a way that my wife could have joined us for lunch? The reality was that nobody in the town knew me anyway. But a much deeper reality surfaced in my heart: if future opportunities like this came up, I would make certain to have another person present, a course of action that I have followed since that time.

REMEMBER GOD'S FAITHFULNESS TO YOU

With the all the pressure we experience to be somebody, to have everything, it's easy to forget how faithful God has been to us. We get so caught up in what we don't have that we fail to recognize what we do. We get so uptight about what we haven't accomplished that we forget all about the great things God has enabled us to do.

When we allow our minds to be flooded with images of those who are what we aren't, or have what we don't, it's easy for us to conclude that we've been overlooked. It's just not fair! God has favored them and forgotten us! Yet the simple truth is God has given us all we need and a whole lot more!

Every one of us can recall numerous ways God has expressed His faithfulness to us. We see it in the "basics" of life, the way He has put a roof over our heads, bread on our tables, and in many cases even the means to enjoy some "extras." But we also see it in more dramatic ways as He has touched our lives with healing, or has clearly saved a loved one from some horrible plight. Had He not been faithful to us, we would never have experienced the good things in life we take for granted. But because He has been faithful, we have been blessed. And we must never lose sight of that fact—never forget God's faithfulness.

Faithfulness in our lives, then, echoes the character of God. In addition, the more faithful we are to others, the more they believe in us, count on us, and trust us, desiring to have us as an integral part of their lives. Our own sense of value soars as we realize we are making a positive impact on others.

What wonderful dividends accrue to those who experience and express faithfulness!

◆ POINTS TO PONDER ◆

1. Now that you've read about faithfulness, how would you define it for somebody who doesn't know what it is?

2. What is the relationship between faithfulness to God and faithfulness to people? Can you truly be faithful to God without being faithful to others?

3. Describe a situation when you expected faithfulness but were let down. How did you respond?

4. How can faithfulness in the lives of others inspire your own faithfulness?

5. List specific areas where you struggle with faithfulness: keeping your word, being honest and forthright, staying committed when everything and everybody is telling you to do otherwise.

6. Are there things that you're committed to that don't merit your commitment? Do you need to rework your priorities?

7. What steps can you start taking immediately to begin expressing faithfulness in specific areas where it is difficult for you?

TEST YOURSELF ON FAITHFULNESS

Please READ the following statements and ask yourself, **"Do I agree that this describes me—my thoughts and actions during the last few months?"** Then, CIRCLE a number on the scale (below) from 1 to 10, showing how strongly you disagree or agree that each statement does or does not apply to you. Thus, a "1" means that you totally disagree that this is a strength in your life and a "perfect 10" means that you totally agree that the statement describes one of your strengths.

Totally Disagree	Very Strongly Disagree	Strongly Disagree	Somewhat Disagree	Slightly Disagree	Slightly Agree	Somewhat Agree	Strongly Agree	Very Strongly Agree	Totally Agree
1	2	3	4	5	6	7	8	9	10

1. I often feel confident that God will do what He promised.	1 2 3 4 5 6 7 8 9 10
2. God gives me strength to be faithful in tough times.	1 2 3 4 5 6 7 8 9 10
3. I have learned to wait on the Lord's timing.	1 2 3 4 5 6 7 8 9 10
4. I am a person who completely trusts the Lord to provide.	1 2 3 4 5 6 7 8 9 10
5. Other people say that they see godly faithfulness in me.	1 2 3 4 5 6 7 8 9 10
6. I have often proven that I can be faithful to God's word.	1 2 3 4 5 6 7 8 9 10
TOTAL SCORE (Read directions) =	

SCORE YOURSELF ON FAITHFULNESS

Take each of the numbered responses you circled, and add up the numbers to make a total score. For example, if you answered "6" to all 6

questions, the total would be 36. Write the total in the box below the questions, and also mark the location of your score on the chart below:

SCORING CHART FOR FAITHFULNESS

(Mark a line through the location of your score)

6 10 15 20 **25** 30 **35** 40 41 **42** 43 44 45 **46** 47 48 **49** 55 57 60

INTERPRETING YOUR SCORE: The middle point (42) represents the average score obtained by typical readers. Below-average scores are 35 or less, and those below 25 are extremely low. Above-average scores are 46 or more, and scores above 49 are extremely high.

If your score is below average, discuss your results with a friend and see if you can identify possible areas of improvement in faithfulness.

Chapter Eleven

Holiness has never been the driving force of the majority.
It is, however, mandatory for anyone who wants to enter the kingdom.

ELISABETH ELLIOT

"You shall be holy, for I the LORD your God am holy."

GOD

Holiness.

It is by no means a neutral word. One way or another, everybody reacts to it. With or without a relationship with God, most people have formed some sort of concept about what holiness means.

...A guru who hangs out on a mountaintop, eating birdseed and dispensing words of wisdom.

...Recollections of a saintly grandma.

...Memories of being whacked with a ruler for acting up in class. Was that what God looked like? Angry face...thick eyebrows pointed to the center...forehead pursed. Was that what it meant to be holy?

We all could put our own spin on "holiness," and the impressions, memories, and emotions bound up with the term in our minds.

But one thing is certain. God expects His people to be holy. In fact, He demands it: "You shall be holy, for I the LORD your God am holy" (Leviticus 19:2). The fact that He repeats the command in the New Testament (1 Peter 1:16) is ample evidence He means business. Apparently God is not offering cafeteria-style Christianity, where we may choose the things we desire and pass up the rest; some things are going to be on our trays whether we select them or not. And holiness will be among them!

The usual definitions of holiness aren't hard to comprehend. Essentially it is defined as "living a godly life," a life dedicated to God, set apart, and pure. A holy life stands out because it stands up for the things of God.

So far, so good.

The problem is, how do you develop that kind of life? Even the apostle Paul found himself doing things he didn't want to do—and not doing the things he desired to do. If it was nearly impossible for *him* to live a holy life, what chance do we have?

THE PLOT THICKENS

When you get to the heart of many books and articles about holiness, you find them taking one of two approaches: I call them the "grit-and-go" and the "hope-it-happens" methods.

Some say that if you're going to live a holy life you need to trust God, tighten your belt, roll up your sleeves, grit your teeth, and get to work on your daily lifestyle. Certainly you have the Holy Spirit to help you in the process, but it's a long, hard struggle. And sometimes you fail.

On the other hand, a few link holiness to a single, dramatic spiritual experience. *Boom! You're there.* You trust God, pray hard, and in a moment in time, holiness simply *happens*. And having become holy, from that point on, you never sin again. Wow!

Unfortunately neither approach gets you where you want to go.

When you're forced to be holy, motivated by guilt, failure, or threat of death, jail, or damnation, you'll only keep trudging along in that direction as long as a hammer remains poised above your head. But take the hammer away, and…well, all bets are off.

Wasn't that true for God's people in the Bible? As long as a lawgiver was present, they followed the rules, but take the lawgiver/judge/king away, and "everyone did what was right in his own eyes." They didn't respect God's laws in their hearts at all. It's that *sin* thing again. It's hard work to pull off holiness when it's such *hard work*! Grit-n-go won't get you there.

That leaves you the radical spiritual event, that great watershed occurrence when holiness descends from heaven like a sky-blue mantle around your shoulders.

Nice idea, but…how many perfect people have you met? Either there aren't any (effectively ruling out the spiritual event option), or perhaps you've never really met one. And when you think you have, you'll come to find out later you just didn't know him well enough. He wasn't wholly holy after all!

Still, God expects us to be holy. And when we have a personal relationship with Jesus and want to follow Him, we truly desire our lives to look like His. *So how does it happen?*

Stay with me for a page or two…I think the answer might surprise you.

THE POWER OF AN IMAGE

God Himself provides the means to cultivate holiness, and whatever work it takes on our part becomes a blessing rather than drudgery. Long ago He laid out a plan in His Word that made holiness both attractive and attainable.

Attractive. Attainable. Did you ever associate those words with holiness? Possibly not. But that's the Bible's take on it. In fact, Scripture makes holiness so appealing, so desirable, that we find ourselves drawn to lives of holiness.

Catch that? Not driven, but *drawn.* We go there because we want to, not because we have to.

We've all heard the expression, "a picture's worth a thousand words," and we've all experienced the truth of it. We've been captivated, stunned, delighted, disgusted, seduced, frightened, challenged—you name it—but profoundly affected by images. These potent images have staying power, a power that transcends time and place. Shut your eyes, and you see them all over again. They are indelibly etched in your memory.

My wife and I have enjoyed many summer sunsets together through the years—some so outrageously intense they stopped us in our tracks, the sky ablaze with swaths of yellow and swatches of coral, fuchsia, and scarlet shouting, "Look at me!" We just had to say something, express our delight, because talking about it made it even more delicious.

That's the way it is with images—they're powerful. Whether they are literal pictures like photographs or paintings, or mental pictures that capture your mind, they grab you emotionally. They demand a response. TV advertisers play to that. Newscasters rely on it.

Images remind and direct you to understand something, believe something, do something, buy something, be something. Depending on the clarity, desirability, and intensity of these visions, they dictate the choices we make and the directions we take.

It may be an image of ourselves fifty pounds lighter, or sipping iced tea on the veranda of our estate, sitting in the corner office with the commanding view of the city, or walking down an aisle of a church on a sunny June afternoon with a certain someone.

Ever wonder how anybody could decide to strap explosives around his waist and blow himself up in the middle of a crowded street? The simple truth is it has everything to do with an image—in this case a compelling vision of the future. The image that captivates his mind is that of paradise, an eternal existence so enchanting it becomes more vibrant, more attractive than the present. The life he is living now looks bleak compared to such a fabulous future. If just one explosive act is the difference between being here and being there, why not press the button?

Images are having a powerful effect on your life right now. Are they helping or hurting you, building you up or tearing you down? How are they affecting the quality of your life? What if God could give you an image so powerful and positive it would move you toward holiness? Ready for this? He can, and He has!

A MOST COMPELLING IMAGE

God gives us a truly life-shaping image in the final few pages of the Bible. Across the centuries this vision has lifted and encouraged all who put their trust in Jesus Christ. The glorified Lord Himself gave this vision to the apostle John, instructing him to record what he was about to see (as best he could), and pass it on so believers through the ages would have a vision of "home," an image that would draw, inspire, and excite them.

From the moment Christians began to take hold of this vision, it did precisely what God intended, whether it was first-century Christians struggling to survive in the depths of the Roman catacombs, or nineteenth-century Christians on plantations in the American South, or untold billions of others who faced persecution or simply confronted the challenges of everyday life.

In the Book of Revelation, John says he was carried away "in the Spirit" to a great and high mountain from which he had the opportunity to view the entire Holy City, the place God's people were destined to inhabit. He had the experience of a lifetime, an up-close-and-personal tour of heaven. As he describes it—or *attempts* to describe it in weak, human language—it was brilliant beyond imagination. The colors were so saturated, the surfaces so dazzling, he was hard pressed for words. Even under the inspiration of the Holy Spirit, the terms he used must have seemed like a rough charcoal sketch of reality.

It's easy to yawn through a portion of Scripture, when your mind and spirit aren't engaged. But God intends for you to be as impacted by this image as John was. In order for that to happen, you need to see this vision through John's eyes and allow it to grip you as it did him. For the next few moments, walk beside him.

As you approach the Holy City, flashes of light dance off the pure jasper walls, arresting your attention. Though immensely deep and seemingly impenetrable, the walls are crystal clear. How many carats is a diamond 1500 miles long and 216 feet thick? Could anything be more magnificent?

Searching for an entry along one of the walls, you spot three gates, each a giant pearl. Makes perfect sense, doesn't it? In contrast to the transparent walls, the perfect lustrous pearls are opaque, allowing you to locate the entrance. You just have to touch them, to run your hands down the silky surface—the very definition of *smooth*. Each gate bears the name of one of the tribes of the children of Israel. Obviously God has plans for those who belong to Him!

While admiring this massive manifestation of pearl, you're jarred by the presence of an angel standing at each pearl gate. And the angels are as spectacular as the structure. Awesome. Powerful. Yet somehow welcoming. Their eyes smile that age-old angelic greeting, *Do not be afraid*.

The city itself rests on twelve foundations, layer upon layer of precious stones. Spanning the entire spectrum from white to purple are stones like jasper bursting with showers of light, sardius glowing fiery red, and lush forest-green emerald. Although every layer of stone is blinding in brilliance, each complements the others. Maybe this is the original template for those sunsets we find so magnificent!

While the colors and quality of these ribbons of radiance cry out for your admiration, you realize you can see right through each layer of stone. *So pure. So clear. Totally transparent.* Such perfection doesn't exist on planet Earth.

Passing through the gate, the sight of the City pulls the air right out of your lungs. Your jaw drops as you realize the City—massive beyond finite comprehension—is *pure gold.* Like the other materials that comprise the City, this gold is so flawless and pure it is clear as glass. The clarity of the surface creates the illusion of floating on air, and the holy ground you are standing on bids you to remove your shoes.

Everything in the City points in one direction—to a throne that defies description. If the walls, gates, angels, foundation, buildings, and street are staggering, they pale in comparison to the throne and its Occupant. Are there superlatives expansive enough to describe a throne occupied by the One whose hand spans the universe? Can you capture in words the fathomless beauty of the One who created from nothing the very colors with which He paints the sunsets? But there's more.

Spilling forth from the base of the throne is a river with sparks of light dancing off the surface as it moves away from the throne. Not a leaf floating on it, it's crystal clear. Flowing down the middle of the golden street, the river is lined with trees bearing fresh fruit each month of the year. "Trees of Life" they are called. Although there was only one such tree in the Garden of Eden, here there are rows of them—an orchard of life!

Your eyes naturally follow the flow of the river back to its point of origin. Seated on the throne is God Himself! This is His throne room, His Holy City! The light emanating from the throne blinds you, brighter than the sun in a clear summer sky, brighter than unfading lightning. You can't gaze directly at it. This is God's glory, the glory that was like a consuming fire on the mountain where Moses received the Ten

Commandments. This is the glory that lights the Holy City, where there is no sun or moon or source of light except God Himself.

Suddenly the purity and clarity of everything makes sense. The foundation, the walls, the buildings in the City, the street and river are all so pure they are completely clear. *Nothing obstructs the view of God!* When you look at the city, you don't focus on the city, you focus on God in its midst. When you look at the street, the river, the stones of the foundation, your eyes aren't drawn to them. As incredibly beautiful as they are, they don't call attention to themselves.

Instead, you look right through them.

To see Him.

His radiance illuminates everything, inviting you right to the Source.

God has given us this consuming image to beckon us toward a life that looks like His. Holiness consists not merely of working hard to be a better person, but of being so drawn to the glory, beauty, purity, and majesty of God that like all the elements of the Holy City, you desire to be transparent to Him. You want nothing in your life to call attention to itself, to draw attention away from Him. Caught up in His vision, your desire is for people to see Him when they look at you...not because they see Him in you, but because they see Him *through* you.

Holiness, then, is simply *transparency to God.*

John, the one whose earthly eyes had been privileged to drink in heavenly visions, characterizes a life lived for the Lord this way:

> Beloved, now we are children of God; and it has not yet been revealed what we shall be, but we know that when He is revealed, we shall be like Him, for we shall see Him as He is. And everyone who has this hope in Him purifies himself, just as He is pure. (1 John 3:2–3)

We cultivate lives that are clearer and purer because we can't imagine settling for anything less.

This vision is the greatest help we have for a life of holiness. But as long as we're in the neighborhood, we should look around at other valuable things to consider on the subject.

THE PULL OF PURITY

Think about it...the purer your life becomes, the more you draw people to God. They see through you and catch a glimpse of Him in His splendor and beauty, in His mercy and peace. That's how purity works—it's appealing. Although we may not think about it consciously, we all desire it. When we're thirsty for a drink of water, we don't want any old water. We want *pure* water. If we didn't care, we would all swig water right out of the tap instead of emptying our wallets for the latest, greatest, and *purest* bottled water from some spring on the backside of the Alps.

Perish the thought that any of us would ever need a blood transfusion, but if we did, would we be willing to settle for just any blood? Are you kidding? It would have to be *pure* blood. Certifiably so. Blood that was even "a little contaminated" could mean the difference between life and death.

It doesn't matter whether we're talking about gold or fragrances or soap—the purer, the better. The purer, the more attractive. Just as it is with things, so with people. The purer, the more attractive. But don't misunderstand: what's so appealing about purity is God, not us. Purity calculated to impress people or draw attention to ourselves wouldn't really be purity at all!

As we see the positive effect of purity in our lives, we can't imagine tolerating anything that detracts from it. Its allure is that strong! As our lives become increasingly purer, they also become clearer. As the impurities are removed, others can see Him through us. The expression, "I can see right through you," isn't a bad word to receive—if what they're seeing through you is God.

ALL THE TOOLS WE NEED

Thankfully, God has given us all the tools we need for clear, pure lives. To begin with, when we confess Jesus Christ as Lord our sins are forgiven, and we receive a brand-new life. We are cleansed of unrighteousness as we confess our sins, and God then gives us what we need to make our lives transparent to Him.

He gives us His written Word to help transform our lives: "The words of the LORD are pure words, like silver tried in a furnace of earth, purified seven times.... Your word is very pure; therefore Your servant loves it" (Psalms 12:6; 119:140). As we commit His Word to memory, allowing it to shape our thoughts, it does a work of purification in us.

He has given us His Spirit to teach, guide, and empower us. Jesus said: "But the Helper, the Holy Spirit, whom the Father will send in My name, He will teach you all things, and bring to your remembrance all things that I said to you" (John 14:26). Peter elaborates on how this works, noting that our souls are purified "in obeying the truth through the Spirit" (1 Peter 1:22).

Ever wonder why you have a twinge of conscience when you receive too much change at the grocery store and could walk out with nobody being the wiser? The Holy Spirit is tapping you on the shoulder to remind you of God's truth and life. He wants you to live in victory, not to lay yourself open to the condemnation of the enemy of your soul. And when we live our lives in the Spirit, there's a fantastic guarantee: "I say then: Walk in the spirit, and you shall not fulfill the lust of the flesh" (Galatians 5:16). How about that!

He has given us the refreshing power of His blood when we inadvertently allow a bug to land on the windshield of our life (or intentionally drive into one!). "If we confess our sins, He is faithful and just to forgive us our sins and to cleanse us from all unrighteousness" (1 John 1:9).

The point is we don't have to play "work-up" in order to experience holiness. God not only offers us an image that carries us along, He also gives us the tools that help us cultivate it continually.

HABITS HELPFUL TO HOLINESS

Finally, as we immerse ourselves in His truth, we find God has identified habits to build into our lives that are helpful for the development of holiness. Some of the most powerful of these are as follows:

- Present your body as a living sacrifice. (Romans 12:1)
- Hide God's Word in your heart. (Job 22:21–22; Psalm 119:11; 2 Timothy 3:16–17)
- Seek and set your mind on those things which are above. (Colossians 3:1–2, Philippians 4:8)
- Forget what's behind you and reach forward to what's ahead. (Philippians 3:13–14)
- Take thoughts captive to Christ. (2 Corinthians 10:4–5)
- Pray without ceasing. (1 Thessalonians 5:17)
- Walk in the Spirit. (Galatians 5:16–17)
- Fellowship with the faithful. (Ephesians 5:18–21; Hebrews 10:24–25)
- Cast all your cares on the Lord. (1 Peter 5:7)
- Seek to serve Him. (Matthew 20:25–28)

Imagine having a life of holiness, transparent to the radiance and splendor of God, a life so pure and clear that others see Him through you. That's the net result of living a life of godly character. Holiness doesn't have to be wishful thinking on your part, nor does it have to be forced by the Holiness Police! As you are caught up in the magnificence of God and His future, cultivating the qualities of godly character won't be a *have to*, it will be a *get to*. Fix your mind and heart on *home*. That's where you're headed! Then let that image shape the way you live.

Truly, it's all about Him.

◆ POINTS TO PONDER ◆

1. Describe your thoughts about *holiness* before reading this chapter. When you read, "You shall be holy, for I the LORD your God am holy," how did you respond? Was it something you thought you could attain? What helped you? What got in your way?

2. When you hear terms like "holy Joe" or "Miss Goody Two-shoes," or overhear people snicker about a student's commitment to "purity," do you feel more like being holy, or blending in with the crowd? How can this new perspective on holiness change your feelings?

3. What have you done about *holiness* in your life thus far?

4. Reflect on the power of images. What are some of the popular images that define or strongly affect your life?

5. Read Revelation 21:9–22:5. Allow yourself to *be there* in your mind. What things stand out to you particularly? What is the overall impression?

6. Have you ever considered the fact that God gave us this image to draw us into His life? Do you look forward to eternity in heaven? What do you imagine you will be doing?

7. Consider the idea that *holiness* is *transparency to God*. What does that mean? How would that look in your life? What are the practical implications? If you would find a fly in your soup disgusting, does sin in your life look any better?

8. Think through the idea that purity is appealing. Highlight several ways this is true. How does this relate to the choices people make today about lifestyle issues—e.g., living together out of marriage, getting involved in addictive habits, etc.?

9. God has clearly given us tools to help us cultivate holiness. How does each help enable it to become reality?

10. Among the habits of holiness, which ones are most important to you right now?

TEST YOURSELF ON HOLINESS

Please READ the following statements and ask yourself, **"Do I agree that this describes me—my thoughts and actions during the last few months?"** Then, CIRCLE a number on the scale (below) from 1 to 10, showing how strongly you disagree or agree that each statement does or does not apply to you. Thus, a "1" means that you totally disagree that this is a strength in your life and a "perfect 10" means that you totally agree that the statement describes one of your strengths.

Totally Disagree	Very Strongly Disagree	Strongly Disagree	Somewhat Disagree	Slightly Disagree	Slightly Agree	Somewhat Agree	Strongly Agree	Very Strongly Agree	Totally Agree
1	2	3	4	5	6	7	8	9	10

1. I am transparent in revealing my sin to God.	1 2 3 4 5 6 7 8 9 10
2. I am dedicated to staying pure.	1 2 3 4 5 6 7 8 9 10
3. I feel that God has set me apart for a holy purpose.	1 2 3 4 5 6 7 8 9 10
4. I can easily control myself to act holy in all situations.	1 2 3 4 5 6 7 8 9 10
5. Other people say often that they see God's Spirit in me.	1 2 3 4 5 6 7 8 9 10
6. I am good at maintaining holiness in my relationships.	1 2 3 4 5 6 7 8 9 10
TOTAL SCORE (Read directions) =	

SCORE YOURSELF ON HOLINESS

Take each of the numbered responses you circled, and add up the numbers to make a total score. For example, if you answered "7" to all 6

questions, the total would be 42. Write the total in the box below the questions, and also mark the location of your score on the chart below:

SCORING CHART FOR HOLINESS

(Mark a line through the location of your score)

6 15 20 25 **30** 35 36 **37** 38 39 40 41 42 43 **44** 45 46 47 48 49 50 51 52 53 54 **55** 56 57 58 **59** 60

INTERPRETING YOUR SCORE: The middle point (44) represents the average score obtained by typical readers. Below-average scores are 37 or less, and those below 30 are extremely low. Above-average scores are 55 or more, and scores above 59 are extremely high.

If your score is below average, discuss your results with a friend and see if you can identify possible areas of improvement in holiness.

Chapter Twelve

*Love is the only force capable
of transforming an enemy into a friend.*

MARTIN LUTHER KING, JR.

*Love cures people—both the ones who give it
and the ones who receive it.*

KARL MENNINGER

So...how's your love life?

You don't approve of the question? Too brash, maybe? Too in-your-face? Then let me put it this way: *What* is your love life?

I really don't intend that to be a trick question—tricky as it may sound. The problem lies in the definition of "love." It means almost anything, and because of that, it means almost nothing.

We love our dog.

We love our vacation.

We love the new paint job on the house.

We make love.

We take love offerings at church.

We hope our spouse will love the birthday gift we purchased.

And don't you just *love* the way your third grader sang "God Bless America!"

So tell me: What does "love" mean, anyway?

Kids think they have a bead on it. One little girl said, "Love is that first feeling you feel before all the bad stuff gets in the way." Another remarked, "Love is when a girl puts on perfume and a boy puts on shaving cologne and they go out and smell each other." Perhaps the best understanding of all is from the little fellow who said, "Love is when you go out to eat and give somebody most of your French fries without making them give you any of theirs." Does love get much better than that?

SHADES OF MEANING

While the man on the street might not agree, the New Testament is actually the best place to gain our understanding of what love really means.

The New Testament was written in street-level Greek, a form of the language existing approximately 300 years before—and after—the earthly life of Jesus. Some say it was the most precise language ever to communicate human thinking. In that language, there are four words for love, each distinct from one another.[1]

Family Love

The first word for love, *storge*, describes love within a family. You might not choose your sister as your best friend, but you love her nonetheless. While the actual word itself doesn't appear on the pages of the New Testament, a compound form of it does. Paul characterized the ungodly as *unloving* (i.e., "without natural affection"), a negative form of this word.

Brotherly Love

Certainly we're all familiar with a second word for love: *philia*. *Philanthropy*, the unselfish concern for the welfare of others, derives its meaning from this word. This form of love is a true and deep affection for others. It's the word Jesus chose to describe His love for John ("the disciple whom Jesus *loved*," John 20:2), and Lazarus ("he whom You *love*," John 11:3).

Erotic Love

Today's culture needs no introduction to the third term for love. *Eros* primarily refers to physical expressions of intimacy...sexual love. So much of contemporary "love talk" derives from this word. Our word *erotic* comes from *eros*. This particular word for love never appears in the New Testament—but its meaning totally dominates our understanding of the subject today!

Notice that all three words are infused with feeling. If we love somebody with *storge, philia,* or *eros,* we have positive, warm feelings about them.

But there is a fourth type of love.

A love that transcends feelings altogether.

A love that exists apart from feelings and in spite of them.

Transcendent Love

In the New Testament, the word used for the deepest, richest form of love is *agape*. In its noun and verb forms, *agape* appears over 250 times! Perhaps because it was such an unused and innocuous word in classical Greek, the early Christians drew it into their street-level vocabulary and infused it with a much more profound meaning to state their understanding of God's love. It came to describe not only God's love, but love on a human level that reflects His love. This God-style love is *a deliberate commitment to seek the highest good of another*, regardless of whether I actually like him, regardless of whether I am attracted to her. It is "unconquerable benevolence, invincible good will."[1]

This is a deliberate act, a choice.

I am acting on a principle, not feelings, to guide my behavior. As Margaret Anderson once said, "In real love you want the other person's good. In romantic love you want the other person."

When it comes to God-style love, I may not like somebody; I may even find his behavior reprehensible. But I can still love him. In my relationship with him I can mirror God's love for me, His deliberate commitment to seek my highest good.

God-style love calls for commitment. It is selfless. It isn't about me! That means I make a commitment to love regardless of how it is received, regardless of whether it is reciprocated. It stands regardless. The response to this love—whatever it may be—doesn't nullify my commitment. Though stated tongue-in-cheek, Johann von Goethe once remarked, "If I love you, what business is it of yours?"

When we understand God-style love, it helps us figure out why people misuse the word *love* so often, even in relationship to God. To clear up some of the misconceptions, let's consider nine truths about God-style love.

#1: IT IS EMPOWERED BY THE HOLY SPIRIT

There is no way we can express God-style love apart from the Holy Spirit. Be honest: even *with* the Holy Spirit it can be a challenge! There's a reason why Scripture lists love as a "fruit of the Spirit"—it flows directly from Him, through us, to another person.

Before he was filled with God's Spirit, Peter wouldn't have been caught dead hanging out with Gentiles. But as a direct result of being empowered by God's Spirit on Pentecost, he suddenly became open to everything God wanted to do in and through his life—even when that meant hanging out with Gentiles! What he would never have done on his own, he did joyfully through God's Holy Spirit.

When you've been the object of gossip, when you've been treated unfairly or even maliciously, is it possible to love the one responsible? In my personal experience it can *only* happen when I depend on the

Holy Spirit to supply God-style love.

I frankly don't know of any other way.

In the strength of the Holy Spirit, I can seek that person's highest good, even though my feelings aren't exactly warm and fuzzy! It is also the strength of the Holy Spirit that motivates and empowers me to seek restoration of broken relationships.

#2: IT CARES FOR THE UNLOVELY AND THE UNLOVABLE

In the Sermon on the Mount Jesus said: "But I say to you, love your enemies, bless those who curse you, do good to those who hate you, and pray for those who spitefully use you and persecute you" (Matthew 5:44).

Try accomplishing *that* in your own strength.

Jesus deliberately committed Himself to seek the highest good of others—whether close friends, tax collectors, lepers, or sinners and rebels of any description. He even loved those who crucified Him. All of them. God-style love moved Him to challenge the religious elite, because He sought their highest good. Their decisions put them directly at odds with God's best for their lives, and Jesus cared too much to let them carry on unchecked. God-style love is no respecter of persons!

Caring for those who care for us takes no effort at all. But when we find someone offensive? When they reject us, mock us, or don't meet our standards? Understand this: loving somebody God's way doesn't mean you have him over for a barbeque; *it means where your lives intersect, you do what you can to encourage his greatest good.* God will take care of the details.

#3: IT IS SINCERE

The apostle Paul couldn't have stated it more clearly: "Let love be without hypocrisy" (Romans 12:9). The Message paraphrase renders the same verse: "Love from the center of who you are; don't fake it." We all know about manipulation. We recognize how easy it is to use others to meet our objectives. When we are committed to seeking another's highest good, there's no room for that.

Who can't recall feeling set up because of another's hypocrisy? We've all encountered Jekyll/Hyde individuals, sweet as strawberry rhubarb pie to our face, but altogether different behind our back.

There's a lesson here for all of us. We don't want our lives to work like that, hiding behind a facade of phony affection while we watch for an opportunity to expose another's dirty laundry. Our challenge is to respond to betrayal with God-style love, and in our relationships with others to be sincere and real. Remember, we're committed to seek their best!

#4: IT HOLDS TO CLEAR STANDARDS

God-style love has absolute standards. Remember the definition? It is a deliberate commitment to seek the highest good of another. You can't seek "the highest good" if there is no standard to determine *higher* and *lower*. Jesus kept the standard of God's commandments, and He expects us to follow in His steps: "If you keep My commandments, you will abide in My love, just as I have kept My Father's commandments and abide in His love" (John 15:10).

Although God would have it otherwise, the lack of absolutes in society today has bled into the church. Since most people in our culture don't think truth is absolute, it's easy for Christians to tag along with the majority. You can see the telltale signs everywhere.

Consider the subject of divorce. Those who have a personal relationship with Christ divorce as often as those who don't. Yet God's highest good for marriage is clearly different. In a discussion about divorce with some religious officials, Jesus said, "Haven't you read the Scriptures?... They record that from the beginning 'God made them male and female…. This explains why a man leaves his father and mother and is joined to his wife, and the two are united into one.' *Since they are no longer two but one, let no one separate them, for God has joined them together"* (Matthew 19:4–6, NLT, emphasis mine).

Jesus further clarified that Moses only allowed for divorce because of the hardness of people's hearts! (See Matthew 19:8.) Just because somebody had lowered the standard, that neither made it right nor God's best. Yet isn't it true that even Christians are increasingly lowering the bar on divorce, finding more and more situations where it's acceptable?

Another subject to think about is sexual purity before marriage. We all know society abandoned that standard long ago, and now Christians by the droves have followed suit. Twenty years ago a couple would have been mortified to admit to their pastor they were living together outside marriage. Now they don't seem to care who knows. Isn't everybody living that way these days?

As a pastor, when I become aware that a couple is living together, it's tempting to look the other way, allowing them to feel comfortable, and remain in our church. But if I did, I wouldn't be loving them God-style, seeking their highest good. God's Word is clear on the subject of marriage, as well as sexual relationships outside of marriage. And secular statistics reinforce everything He says. Divorce wreaks havoc on children, and when a couple begins their physical relationship prior to marriage, the chance their marriage will fail is overwhelming. That's one of many reasons why God-style love has clear standards.

#5: IT TELLS THE TRUTH

God-style love always tells the truth, communicated with both compassion and candor. "Therefore, putting away lying, 'Let each one of you speak truth with his neighbor,' for we are members of one another" (Ephesians 4:25). If we don't tell the truth, how can we hope to encourage another's best?

Recently I was a guest at a dinner featuring several speakers. One of them had been in the media recently due to the stand he took on marriage as a union between one man and one woman—period! Because of his biblical position, he had garnered a significant amount of negative press. The program that evening had nothing to do with same-sex marriage, but the folks who supported that decided to show up and protest anyway. One woman held up a large sign proclaiming in bold letters, *My God does not hate!*

The implications of her sign were clear: (a) the guest speaker was a hate-monger, (b) anyone who listened to him was also a hate-monger, and (c) God loved any and everything, particularly what this woman supported personally.

This woman may have been sincere, but she was sincerely wrong. Her sign was entirely false! The truth is, God hates all sorts of things. In just one passage of Proverbs alone it says: "These six things the LORD hates, yes, seven are an abomination to Him" (Proverbs 6:16). Elsewhere we read God hates abominations, false gods, workers of iniquity, deceitful people, and divorce.

Why? Because He is committed to seeking the highest good of every man, woman, and child, and none of these things will bring that about. And it doesn't help anybody to smile and pass it off as "whatever." God-style love tells the truth.

#6: IT PAYS WHATEVER IT COSTS

Just hours before His death, Jesus said: "Greater love has no one than this, than to lay down one's life for his friends" (John 15:13). His love for the world cost Jesus His life, and it cost God the Father His one-and-only Son. God-style love pays whatever it costs to gain another's highest good.

In the prison memoirs *Against All Hope,* Armando Valladares told the story of a prisoner named Gerardo, known to most of the other prisoners simply as the "Brother of the Faith." In situation after situation, when his fellow prisoners were unable to handle their difficult assignments, though he was a small man, Gerardo would step in and get their job done along with his own, so they wouldn't be beaten. And if it happened that the guards decided to beat them anyway, somehow he would manage to take their punishment upon himself.

Valladares describes one such situation when the guards were venting their fury on the prisoners with machetes and bayonets. "Suddenly one prisoner, as the guards rained blows on his back, raised his arms and face to the sky and shouted, 'Forgive them, Lord, for they know not what they do!' There was not a trace of pain, not a tremble in his voice; it was as though it were not his back the machete was lashing, over and over again, shredding his skin. The brilliant eyes of the 'Brother of the Faith' seemed to burn; his arms open to the sky seemed to draw down pardon for his executioners."[2]

The Brother of the Faith was willing to pay the price of God-style love, putting his body on the line while seeking God's best for friend and foe alike.

While most of us will never be called upon to express love to this extent, seeking the highest good of others will cost us. It may be time, money, convenience, misunderstanding, or popularity, but there will be a price. God-style love will pay whatever it costs.

#7: IT GIVES WHAT IT HAS BEEN GIVEN

The apostle John speaks for all who have life in Christ: "We know how much God loves us, and we have put our trust in him. God is love, and all who live in love live in God, and God lives in them" (1 John 4:16, NLT).

Anyone who has trusted Christ for life has experienced God-style love personally. That person knows what it's like to be loved even though he's unlovable. We know it in our heads because we have believed His promises, and we feel it in our hearts because He continues to bless and encourage us. God-style love is not just an interesting theory to us.

When we are saturated in His love, it becomes a natural response to pass it on. We love because we are loved. Just as God doesn't base His love for us on our performance (praise be to God!), neither do we. We are aware we all have our shortcomings, so we give gratefully from the inexhaustible supply of love extended to us.

Whenever I run across somebody struggling with accepting or loving another because of "his sin," I often ask that person to recall his own challenges in life. I ask him to remember how his life looked when God reached out to him. When we have that perspective, realizing all have sinned and fallen short of God's glory, it makes it infinitely easier to pass on to others the same God-style love that has been shown to us.

#8: IT NEVER GIVES UP

In the greatest treatise on God-style love, Paul said simply yet most profoundly, "Love never fails" (1 Corinthians 13:8). God-style love never quits, never throws in the towel, never walks away. The person we are committed to may let us down, turn their back on us, or even walk away from the relationship. But we keep on loving.

Remember the parable of the prodigal son? It might more accurately be described as the parable of *the loving father* (see Luke 15:11–32). You recall the story. A young man demands his inheritance from his father long before it's due. Dad agrees to give it to him, allowing him to do with it whatever he chooses. With breakneck speed he fritters it away and is left penniless and starving. Overwhelmed, discouraged, and

deservedly down on himself, his heart turns toward home. Not knowing what else to do, he returns—hoping only that his father will allow
him to be a hired servant.

But things turn out quite differently.

As the young man approaches the house, it's as if his dad had been
waiting for him the whole time he was gone. His father runs to meet
him, receiving him with open arms.

At the heart of the parable is the love of the father, a love that
never, never gives up. That's the way God-style love operates: it refuses
to quit! Isn't that how God has treated all of us? We've all had our
"prodigal" seasons when we wasted our time, our resources, and the
gifts God has given us. Yet when we turned our hearts toward home,
we found our heavenly Father with arms wide open waiting to draw us
to Himself anew.

That is exactly the kind of love that we all get to extend, a love that
never gives up.

#9: IT IS THE BASIS FOR A GODLY LIFE

Paul's summary statement to the great love chapter reads: "And now
abide faith, hope, love, these three; but the greatest of these is love"
(1 Corinthians 13:13).

If humility is the foundation for all the qualities of godly character,
then God-style love is their sum. When all these qualities work
together, they enhance one another and make unique contributions to
the expression of God-style love.

I can't think about our Lord's apostles without being struck by the
depth of their love. Virtually every one of those men died a violent
death because of his God-style love, a total commitment to seek God's
best for all His people. God's love motivated them to do what they did
and kept them going when they could have given up.

As we commit ourselves to seek the highest good of others, to express God-style love in every relationship, our lives will conform more and more to the character of Christ. That kind of life brings God glory, receives His blessing…and His smile.

SATISFACTION GUARANTEED

God's smile.

My friend, we were *made* for it! We were created for God's pleasure, for His companionship, for His touch on our daily lives, for being caught up in His plans and purposes. We could seek to fill that God-sized empty place in a million ways for a million years and never, never find a handle on genuine, bone-deep satisfaction—apart from Christ.

In one way or another, everybody seeks satisfaction. And so few…so very, very few find that path to lifelong contentment and fulfillment.

It doesn't have to be that way! In fact, Jesus Christ, the God-man, the One who came so that we "might have life, and have it more abundantly," *guarantees* satisfaction to everyone who will simply take Him at His word: "Blessed are those who hunger and thirst for righteousness, for they shall be satisfied."

Lots of people make lots of promises about lots of things…but not one of those people is infallible, unchangeable, or all-powerful. And not one of them can love you with the blazing, eternal love of the One who formed and created you for Himself.

You can take God's guarantee to the bank.

In fact, you can stake your very life on it.

◆ POINTS TO PONDER ◆

1. Think about the way you use the word "love." Highlight different categories of usage—the way you *love* a hobby, *love* your spouse, *love* a sunset, etc. What is the difference in what you mean by love in each context?

2. Consider the four different words for love in the Greek language. Reflect on the way such distinctions could help you in using this powerful word.

3. What is "God-style love," and what sets it apart from the others?

4. Read Romans 5:8. What does that teach us about the relationship between God-style love and feelings?

5. What are the main truths about God-style love you struggle with personally? What action steps can you take to work on that?

6. What is the difference between God-style love and *affirmation*? *Acceptance*? Can you truly love somebody God-style and not affirm his behavior? How do standards enter in?

7. Look at Ephesians 4:11–16, especially verse 15. Among the marks of maturity is speaking the truth in love. Can you remember a situation where telling the truth in love created problems? Would it have been better for you to be quiet? If not, why not?

8. Read the Parable of the Prodigal Son (Luke 15:11–32). Consider each character carefully. What do we learn from each one about love?

9. Review the benefits of *God-style love*. As we experience and express God's love:

- It reflects the character of God Himself. (John 13:35)
- It completes His love. (1 John 4:12, 17)
- It provides support and encouragement to others. (Philemon 7)
- It builds up the Body of Christ. (Hebrews 10:24)
- It covers a multitude of sins. (1 Peter 4:8)
- It casts out all fear of where we will spend eternity. (1 John 4:18)

Which are most important to you right now?

TEST YOURSELF ON LOVE

Please READ the following statements and ask yourself, **"Do I agree that this describes me—my thoughts and actions during the last few months?"** Then, CIRCLE a number on the scale (below) from 1 to 10, showing how strongly you disagree or agree that each statement does or does not apply to you. Thus, a "1" means that you totally disagree that this is a strength in your life and a "perfect 10" means that you totally agree that the statement describes one of your strengths.

Totally Disagree	Very Strongly Disagree	Strongly Disagree	Somewhat Disagree	Slightly Disagree	Slightly Agree	Somewhat Agree	Strongly Agree	Very Strongly Agree	Totally Agree
1	2	3	4	5	6	7	8	9	10

1. I often feel love for people that the world calls "unlovable."	1 2 3 4 5 6 7 8 9 10
2. I truly feel God's love every day.	1 2 3 4 5 6 7 8 9 10
3. I am a very loving person.	1 2 3 4 5 6 7 8 9 10
4. I often have feelings of love for lost people of the world.	1 2 3 4 5 6 7 8 9 10
5. I feel God's calling to love my family unconditionally.	1 2 3 4 5 6 7 8 9 10
6. Other people say that they see Jesus' love coming from me.	1 2 3 4 5 6 7 8 9 10
TOTAL SCORE (Read directions) =	

SCORE YOURSELF ON LOVE

Take each of the numbered responses you circled, and add up the numbers to make a total score. For example, if you answered "6" to all 10

questions, the total would be 60. Write the total in the box below the questions, and also mark the location of your score on the chart below:

SCORING CHART FOR LOVE

(Mark a line through the location of your score)

6 20 25 **30 35** 38 39 40 41 42 43 44 45 **46** 47 48 49 50 51 52 53 54 **55** 56 57 58 **59** 60

INTERPRETING YOUR SCORE: The middle point (46) represents the average score obtained by typical readers. Below-average scores are 35 or less, and those below 30 are extremely low. Above- average scores are 55 or more, and scores above 59 are extremely high.

If your score is below average, discuss your results with a friend and see if you can identify possible areas of improvement in love.

Endnotes

Satisfaction

1. Deputy Brett King, "Photo Essay,"*CBS News.com*, 30 April 2005. http://www.cbsnews.com/elements/2005/04/30/in_depth_us/ photoessay692188_0_8_photo.shtml (accessed 6 October 2005).

Humility

1. Jim Collins, *Good to Great: Why Some Companies Make the Leap...and Others Don't* (New York: HarperCollins, 2001), 17–21.

Thankfulness

1. Frances Gardner Hunter, heard by author at talk by Mrs. Hunter, 1974.
2. Gregg Easterbrook, *The Progress Paradox: How Life Gets Better While People Feel Worse* (New York: Random House, 2003), 238.
3. Ibid.
4. Ibid., 239.
5. Robert A. Emmons and Michael E. McCullough, eds., *The Psychology of Gratitude* (Oxford University Press, 2004).
6. Michael E. McCullough, "Psychology Professor Publishes Research on Gratitude," *SMU News*, 21 May 2001.
7. Melanie B. Smith, "Attitude of Gratitude," *The Decatur Daily* (Decatur, AL), Saturday, November 20, 2004.

Contentment

1. Deborah Taylor-Hough, *A Simple Choice: A Practical Guide for Saving Your Time, Money and Sanity* (Belgium, Wisconsin: Champion Press, 2000).

Patience

1. Aron Ralston, *Between a Rock and a Hard Place* (New York: Atria Books, 2004).

Peace

1. Mark Levine, "Saving Face," *New York Magazine*, June 14, 2004.

Joy

1. Charlie and Lucy Wedemeyer, taken from "Words of Encouragement" on the DVD "Courage to Live," 2003, produced by Don Mates and Suzanne Maurer.
2. Ibid.

Love

1. William Barclay, *New Testament Words* (Louisville, Kentucky: Westminster Press, 1964), 21-22.
2. Armando Valladares, *Against All Hope* (New York: Alfred A. Knopf, 1986), 254.